At Issue

Is American Society Too Materialistic?

Other books in the At Issue series:

Are Americans Overmedicated?

Are America's Wealthy Too Powerful?

Are Chain Stores Ruining America?

Are Conspiracy Theories Valid?

Are Cults a Serious Threat?

Can Democracy Succeed in the Middle East?

Does Equality Exist in America?

Does Outsourcing Harm America?

Heroin

How Can Gang Violence Be Prevented?

Interracial Relationships

Is Factory Farming Harming America?

Is Iran a Threat to Global Security?

Is Media Violence a Problem?

Is the American Dream a Myth?

Is the Political Divide Harming America?

Physician-Assisted Suicide

Racial Profiling

Satanism

What Limits Should Be Placed on Presidential Power?

What Rights Should Illegal Immigrants Have?

The Wireless Society

At Issue

Is American Society Too Materialistic?

Ronnie D. Lankford, Book Editor

GREENHAVEN PRESS

An imprint of Thomson Gale, a part of The Thomson Corporation

THOMSON

GALE

Detroit • New York • San Francisco • New Haven, Conn. • Waterville, Maine • London • Munich

Bonnie Szumski, *Publisher*
Helen Cothran, *Managing Editor*

For more information, contact: Greenhaven Press
27500 Drake Rd.
Farmington Hills, MI 48331-3535
Or you can visit our Internet site at http://www.gale.com

LIBRARY OF CONGRESS CATALOGING-IN-PUBLICATION DATA

Is American society too materialistic? / Ronnie D. Lankford, book editor.
   p. cm. -- (At issue)
  Includes bibliographical references and index.
  0-7377-3395-0 (lib. : alk. paper) 0-7377-3396-9 (pbk. : alk. paper)
  1. Consumption (Economics)--United States. 2. Materialism--United
States--Social aspects. 3. Materialism--United States. I. Lankford,
Ronald D., 1962–. II. At issue (San Diego, Calif.)
  HC110.C6 I79 2007
  339.4'70973--dc22
                                      2006041090

Contents

Introduction

Consumer Debt

In a recent economic downturn, Americans reversed a historical trend. "When times are good," writes Paul J. Lim in *U.S. News & World Report*, "families assume things will be good forever, so they spend more and save less. When times get tough . . . consumers tighten their belts, saving more and borrowing less."[1] In 2000 and 2001, however, amid economic recession, Americans continued to spend as they had spent during more prosperous times. "The truth is," one consumer told Lim, "nobody wants to sacrifice their lifestyle."[2]

It is not surprising, then, that consumer debt in the United States has grown to unprecedented proportions. The percentage of consumer debt rose from 96 percent of disposable income in 2000 to 113 percent in 2004. Overall consumer debt rose from $7 trillion in January 2000 to $9.3 trillion in April 2003. According to the Federal Reserve, that total represents an average of $18,700 of debt per household (the figure includes car payments but excludes mortgages).

Related to consumer debt is the low rate of savings in the United States. Throughout the 1980s the consumer savings rate equaled 10 percent of each dollar earned; by November 2005 the savings rate had dropped to a negative 0.2 percent. "You're seeing a situation," economic consultant Joel Naroff told the *San Francisco Chronicle*, "where the consumers are spending every penny they possibly can and borrowing on top of that."[3]

Credit card debt alone has grown precipitously. Household credit card debt in the United States rose steadily from an average of $7,842 in 2000 to $9,312 in 2004. At the beginning of 2004 the total credit card debt in the United States was $735

7

billion. A heavy share of this debt falls on young consumers between the ages of eighteen and twenty-four, who rely on credit and debit cards to make 50.4 percent of their purchases. "These young consumers so consistently reach for the debit and credit cards," writes Michael Liedtke in the *Houston Chronicle*, "that Visa USA has anointed the age group 'Generation Plastic,' or 'Gen P.'"[4] Some analysts have suggested a cause-and-effect relationship between high debit card use and the current low savings rate: While debit cards, which deduct expenses directly from funds in checking or savings accounts, do not increase individual debt, they do make spending money much easier than saving it.

Why do so many Americans find themselves so deeply in debt? There are many reasons, including gambling, medical bills, job loss, and divorce. But the growth of consumer debt also reveals that Americans are simply unwilling to wait to make many purchases. "Materialism is certainly part of the problem," Jennifer Errick notes in a *New American Dream* newsletter:

> Americans like to shop. We like big stuff and we like lots of it. Everything in our lives is getting bigger, from vehicles and houses to TV screens and bathtubs. Shopping is viewed as patriotic, credit lines arrive and expand in our mailboxes nearly every day, and we are bombarded with ads that tell us to buy our way to security, happiness, friendship, and sex.[5]

By wanting everything and wanting it now, an increasing number of Americans find themselves in a financial bind. Delinquencies in credit card payment climbed to a record 4.81 percent in the spring of 2005. "What's happened to the family," author Amelia Warren Tyagi told the *San Francisco Chronicle*, "is that they have budgeted to the limit of those two incomes. If anything happens—a job loss or an illness—they're stuck."[6] One result of excessive consumer debt is increases in foreclosures and bankruptcy. Personal bankruptcy filings rose from 900,000 in 1995 to 1.6 million in 2004, a trend that ultimately adversely affects all consumers: "The U.S. Chamber of Commerce estimates businesses lose about $40 billion annually to bankruptcies," notes the *Arizona Daily Star*, "passing much of the cost on to consumers."[7]

In 2005 bankruptcy filings reached an all-time high, partly in response to the April passage of the Bankruptcy Abuse Prevention and Consumer Protection Act. The new law, most provisions of which took effect October 17, 2005, makes it more difficult for individuals to eliminate their debt simply by filing for legal bankruptcy status known as Chapter 7. In the ten days before the law took effect, 500,000 individuals claimed bankruptcy. Altogether, over 2 million Americans, one in 53 people, filed for bankruptcy in 2005, resulting in losses to credit providers of over $500 million. Home foreclosures also rose from 76,526 in 2002 to 85,000 in 2005.

No one can predict the future spending and saving habits of the American consumer, but statistics do underline a basic fact of contemporary life in the United States: Consumers have access to more credit than ever. According to the *San Antonio Business Journal*, there are over 785 million credit cards currently in circulation, used to charge $1.5 trillion each year. The number of credit cards is likely to grow, as credit card companies expand their traditional base by aggressively marketing to college and high school students. "Is there a way for Americans to step off of this spending treadmill while still holding on to a sense of economic opportunity?" asks business writer James Surowiecki: "It seems doubtful. After all, the very thing that propels American entrepreneurialism—the idea that with enough cleverness and effort, anything is possible—also fuels American overspending and overindulgence."[8]

Notes

1. Paul J. Lim, "Drowning in Debt?" *U.S. News & World Report*, August 8, 2005.
2. Quoted in Lim, "Drowning in Debt?"
3. Quoted in Tom Abate, "Americans Saving Less than Nothing," *San Francisco Chronicle*, January 8, 2006.
4. Michael Liedtke, "Generation P," *Houston Chronicle*, January 16, 2006.

5. Jennifer Errick, "Debt, Security, and the American Dream," *New American Dream*, January 31, 2006. www.newdream.org.

6. Quoted in Abate, "Americans Saving Less than Nothing."

7. *Arizona Daily Star*, "Overhaul of Federal Bankruptcy Code Means Big Changes for Debtors," September 18, 2005.

8. James Surowiecki, "People of Plenty," *Fast Company*, March 2003. www.findarticles.com/p/articles/mi_kmfas/is_200303/ai_kepm31830.

1

Consumerism Is Harmful

John F. Schumaker

John F. Schumaker is a senior lecturer in clinical psychology at the University of Canterbury and author of The Age of Insanity.

The personal spending of Americans exceeds that of every other nation. Americans are proud of their excess, unaware that their greed for consumer goods creates enormous waste and leads to environmental problems. American materialism has also created psychological distress, leading to more depression, lack of self-esteem, and compulsive disorders. The world, if it wishes to prosper in a healthy and safe way, should resist America's unhealthy model of consumerism.

On a recent visit home to Wisconsin I found myself sitting alone in a crowded shopping mall, feeling the same intangible revulsion that eventually banished me from America. Above me towered a brutish vending machine, complete with celestial chimes, rotating lights and a steely synthesized voice beckoning the assembly of dupes. A miserable young lad approached, dragging the body of his package-laden mother. He searched her eyes repeatedly until she finally fed the machine, got a Rocket Ranger toy and stuck it out to her child.

He slapped it onto the floor and screeched for still another selection. Mom stuffed in more bills until finally the boy was out of choices. "Well, for God's sake, what do you want," she bellowed.

In a confused rage the boy bawled, over and over again, "I want something, I want something, I want something." As I

John F. Schumaker, "Dead Zone," *New Internationalist*, July 2001, p. 34. Copyright © 2001 *New Internationalist Magazine*. Reproduced by permission.

watched the boy I thought that, after all these years, America is still shooting up the town, still digging its heels unnecessarily deep into the precious elements that sustain us, and still making me glad that I now live in New Zealand.

The boy seemed to forewarn of capitalism's psychological dead end where life masquerades as a kaleidoscope of consumer choices. His was the collective voice of mindless consumerism as it has been perfected and amplified in America. It spoke too of the existential loneliness that gnaws at me whenever I return to the "all-consuming society" as some sociologists have come to call America.

Institutionalized Overconsumption

American culture has assigned its fate to institutionalized overconsumption. This radical psycho-economic device lies at the heart of the country's much celebrated economic boom. What we see unfolding in the US is a human tragedy that was foreseen by [American playwright] Thornton Wilder in *The Bridge of San Luis Rey*. There he describes a people who are "drunk with self-gazing and in dread of all appeals that might interrupt their long communion with their own desires." Scratch the surface of the economic boom and you see a grotesque epidemic of desire and greed. This is what America's bold experiment with radical consumerism is all about.

As I sat in the mall that day I wondered what my hero Albert Einstein would think about the patterns of cultural consciousness that are encouraged in present-day America. In an interview he once said: "The ideals which have lighted my way, and time after time given me new courage to face life cheerfully, have been kindness, beauty, and truth. The trite subjects of life—possessions, outward success, luxury—have always seemed contemptible."

Late in his life Einstein expressed grave concerns that trite commercial values were beginning to silence loftier human motivations among Americans and he feared the wider consequences of the social sanctioning of greed. Yet not even he could have foreseen the degree of authority that would eventually be commanded by all things trite.

Scratch the surface of the economic boom and you see a grotesque epidemic of desire and greed.

However, as we all know, the person-as-customer cultural strategy is a sure winner from the standpoint of an economy driven by overconsumption. The percentage of total economic activity that is generated in America from personal spending has reached 70 percent, far more than any other nation.

In a spending showdown, no one is faster or more deadly than Americans. We spend hugely more on ourselves than our closest rival. Private spending is between 50 percent and 90 percent greater than in all major European countries. Over the past five years the savings rate in the US has fallen to a negative rate so that we now spend around $35 billion more than we earn. Virtually all shame has been erased from indebtedness. In 1999 US citizens racked up credit-card debt of $1.5 trillion, while total consumer debt reached a mind-boggling $6 trillion. The one million bankruptcies filed annually due to credit excesses are readily absorbed by an economic system that flourishes on consumer foolhardiness.

Ecological Costs of Overconsumption

When it comes to the physical-waste side of the equation, Americans are leaving Sasquatch-sized footprints. The strategy of overproduction, overspending and overconsumption sees Americans piling up far more solid waste than any other nation. The typical US family of four amasses a seemingly impossible 13 kg [28.6 pounds] of solid waste per day.

Like guns and God, overconsumption has very special meanings to Americans. Most feel proud as well as fortified by the cultural assumption that overindulgence is good for the country. By sheltering them from all the bad news about over-consumption, the US media has suppressed most environmental awareness, even in the face of an impending ecological holocaust. The bulk of the American public accepts the primitive economic reasoning underlying their collective assault on the world's resources. The triumph of consumer consciousness has seen banality and vulgarity anointed with respectability. The utterly superfluous has become a noble pursuit and the quest for personal and intellectual growth is fading quickly. Greed has lost most of its negative connotations.

So just how shallow have we Americans become under the reign of consumerism? In 1970, a large-scale survey of US university students showed that 80 percent of them had as a goal "the development of a meaningful philosophy of life." By 1989, the percentage had fallen to 41 percent. During the same period, the number of those aiming "to be very well off financially" increased from 39 percent to 75 percent—which explains the wholesale shift to studying "marketable" subjects.

The triumph of consumer consciousness has seen banality and vulgarity anointed with respectability.

American-style radical consumerism has succeeded to the point that social analysts now speak of things like "consumer trance" and "ecological dissociation." Take the fascination with sport utility vehicles (SUVs). Who would have thought in these delicate environmental times that the public could be sold a popular mode of transport that consumes one-third more fuel and creates 75 percent more pollution than ordinary cars? And who would have guessed that the average fuel efficiency of US cars in the year 2001 would be less than in the hog-car days of the 1950s and 1960s? Environmentalists have calculated that the SUV fad has caused Americans to waste 70 billion gallons of gasoline in the past 10 years—an immense price for an outdoorsy image.

Overconsumption as National Identity

An article just appeared in my local *Christchurch Mail* newspaper, titled "New Zealand Fails To Measure Up Against United States." Comparing ten economic indicators across the two countries it left no doubt that America was leaving New Zealand in the dust. It is a standing joke that New Zealand is 20 years behind developments in the US. Yet many Kiwis are catching up. Imported SUVs parade through the streets of Auckland, 24-hour shopping is being tested and Kiwis are becoming gradually fatter. But New Zealand has not yet made overconsumption its national pastime and the core of its national identity.

Eighty-five percent of Americans indicated in a recent poll that a "six figure" income would be required to service their yearned-for lifestyle. Yet nearly 30 percent of those actually earning six figures reported that their "basic needs" were not being met. This dizzying degree of consumer desire and the exquisitely concocted discontent underlying it cannot be achieved overnight.

While most societies throughout history have organized themselves in order to curb natural greed, America's devoted consumers are encouraged to respect, nurture and act on the subtlest stirrings of their avarice. As a result materialism has reached fever pitch and continues to rise sharply. In a 1976 survey of US high school students, 38 percent indicated that having "a lot of money" was a primary goal in life. In 1988, the figure had risen to 63 percent. Today one would feel downright silly for even asking if "a lot of money" is important.

Psychological Costs of Overconsumption

Of special concern to mental-health professionals are studies showing that high degrees of materialism have a toxic effect on psychological and social wellbeing. A strong materialist orientation has been associated with diminished life satisfaction, impaired self-esteem, dissatisfaction with friendships and leisure activities, and a predisposition to depression.

Escalating materialism may be the single largest contributor to Western society's tenfold increase in major depression over the past half-century. It certainly features in the worrying rash of "consumption disorders" such as compulsive shopping, consumer vertigo and kleptomania.

Finding an antidote to the Americanization of the world must be the top priority of the international community.

Hyper-materialism also features prominently in the emerging plague of "existential disorders" such as chronic boredom, ennui, jadedness, purposelessness, meaninglessness and alienation. Surveys of therapists reveal that 40 percent of Americans seeking psychotherapy today suffer from these and other complaints, often referred to as all-pervasive "psychic deadness." Once materialism becomes the epicenter of one's life it can be hard to feel any more alive than the lifeless objects that litter the consumer world. In a recent study of US university students, 81 percent of them reported feeling in an "existential vacuum."

And children are on the frontlines of the consumer blitz. An average eight-year-old in the US can list 30 popular brand names. More than 90 percent of 13-year-old girls in one survey listed shopping as their favorite pastime, followed by TV watching. In 1968 US children aged 4–12 spent around $2 billion a year; today they spend nearly $30 billion. And savvy marketers now concentrate on "cradle-to-grave" indoctrination strategies.

The world seems hellbent on following America's lead. But there is nothing useful to be learned from the American Dream in its present hyper-commercialized form. The toxic consciousness that it fosters has transformed the dream into a nightmare. Finding an antidote to the Americanization of the world must be the top priority of the international community.

As a very first step we can discipline ourselves to be critical of all the "positive economic indicators" that we hear about the American economy. We do not want to measure up to the cultural greed and shared mindlessness that has earned America its preeminent economic status.

The footprints of tomorrow's people must be very light indeed. Let it be our job to set an entirely different example that can take us more safely into a highly uncertain future. Buy nothing for a day and try to rise above your sense of cultural failure.

2

Consumerism Creates a Healthy Economy

W. Michael Cox and Richard Alm

W. Michael Cox is a senior vice president and chief economist at the Federal Reserve Bank of Dallas. Richard Alm is a business writer for the Dallas Morning News. Cox and Alm are also the authors of Myths of Rich and Poor: Why We're Better Off than We Think.

Americans have a reputation for being conspicuous consumers, embracing materialism for the sake of materialism. But most Americans also want a balanced life. Although Americans continue to consume more thanks to an efficient consumer-oriented economy, they have also made sacrifices in material gain for less tangible items like leisure time, convenience, and variety. These lifestyle gains, seldom accounted for in economic data like gross domestic product, are the result of a market-based economy, not government or pressure groups. Although the American market is very good at producing consumer goods, it has also played a pivotal role in helping Americans obtain a balanced life.

America's consumer culture is all around us. It's along our highways, studded with shopping malls, fast food joints, and flashy neon signs. It's in our homes, filled with gadgets, furnishings, toys, and closets of clothes, it permeates the media, where ads tell us happiness and sex appeal are as close as the nearest store. It's even within us, at least to the extent that we tie status and identity to the cars we drive, the clothes we wear, and the food we eat.

That's our reputation: a consumer-driven, somewhat crass, shop-'til-you-drop society. As the world's wealthiest nation, we should consume a lot, but the portrait of Americans as consumption crazed misses as much as it captures. We're not working just to acquire more goods and services. Most of us strive for something broader: a balanced life.

Consumption is part of that, of course. We buy myriad things: Chevrolet cars, Sony TV sets, Levi's jeans, Nike sneakers, McDonald's hamburgers, Dell computers. But our wish list doesn't stop there. We also want leisure time, a respite to enjoy life. We want pleasant working conditions and good jobs, so earning a living isn't too arduous. We want safety and security, so we don't live in fear. We want variety, the spice of life. We want convenience, which makes everyday life a little easier. We want a cleaner environment, which enhances health and recreation.

A full description of a balanced life would entail much more, with considerations for family and friends, perhaps even spirituality. Here we want to focus on the components of happiness that clearly depend on the market but are not reflected in the gross domestic product (GDP). Our free enterprise system provides much more than the goods and services we consume; it furnishes ingredients of a balanced life that are often overlooked in discussions of economic performance.

Our free enterprise system provides much more than the goods and services we consume; it furnishes ingredients of a balanced life that are often overlooked in discussions of economic performance.

Capitalism creates wealth. During the last two centuries, the United States became the world's richest nation as it embraced an economic system that promotes growth, efficiency, and innovation. Real GDP per capita tripled from 1900 to 1950; then it tripled again from 1950 to 2000, reaching $35,970.

The wealth didn't benefit just a few. It spread throughout society. For many people, owning a home defines the American Dream, and 68 percent of families now do—the highest percentage on record. Three-quarters of Americans drive their own cars. The vast majority of households possess color televisions (98 percent), videocassette recorders (94 percent), microwave ovens (90 percent), frost-free refrigerators (87 percent), washing machines (83 percent), and clothes dryers (75 percent). In the past decade or so, computers and cell phones have become commonplace.

As people become wealthier, they continue to consume more, but they also look to take care of other needs and wants. They typically choose to forgo at least some additional goods and services, taking a portion of their new wealth in other forms.

Consider a nation that rapidly increases its productive capacity with each passing generation. Workers could toil the same number of hours, taking all of the gains as consumption. They may choose to do so for a while, but eventually they will give up some potential material gains for better working conditions or additional leisure. Hours of work shrink. Workplaces become more comfortable. In the same way, we give up consumption in favor of safety, security, variety, convenience, and a cleaner environment.

Less Work, More Play

In the early years of the Industrial Revolution, most Americans were poor, and they wanted, above all, more goods and services. These factory workers sharply improved their lives as consumers, even though for most of them it meant long hours of toil in surroundings we'd consider abominable today. As

America grew richer, what workers wanted began to change, and leisure became a higher priority.

Few of us want to dedicate every waking hour to earning money. Free time allows us to relax and enjoy ourselves, spend time with family and friends. Higher pay means that each hour of work yields more consumption—in essence, the price for an hour of leisure is going up—but we're still choosing to work less than ever before. . . . Although today we hear stories about harried, overworked Americans who never seem to have enough time, the proportion of time spent on the job has continued to fall. Average weekly hours for production workers dropped from 39 in 1960 to 34 in 2001.

Since 1950 time off for holidays has doubled, to an average of 12 days a year. We've added an average of four vacation days a year. Compared to previous generations, today's Americans are starting work later in life, spending less time on chores at home, and living longer after retirement. All told, 70 percent of a typical American's waking lifetime hours are available for leisure, up from 55 percent in 1950.

Americans may find themselves pressed for time, but it's not because we're working harder than we used to. We're busy having fun.

Even at work, Americans aren't always doing the boss's bidding. According to University of Michigan time diary studies, the average worker spends more than an hour a day engaged in something other than assigned work while on the job. Employees run errands, socialize with colleagues, make personal telephone calls, send e-mail, and surf the Internet. More than a third of American workers, a total of 42 million, access the Internet during working hours. The peak hours for submitting bids on eBay, the popular online auction site, come between noon and 6 p.m., when most Americans are supposedly hard at work.

With added leisure, the United States has turned arts, entertainment, and recreation into a huge industry. Since 1970, attendance per 100,000 people has risen for symphonies, operas, and theaters as well as for national parks and big-league sporting events. The annual Communications Industry Forecast, compiled by New York–based Veronis, Suhler & Associates, indicates that we watch an average of 58 hours of movies at home each year. Yet Americans go out to an average of 5.4 movies a year, up from 4.5 three decades ago.

The number of amusement parks has increased from 362 in 1970 to 1,164 today. The number of health and fitness facilities has more than doubled, to 11,241. Adjusted for inflation, per capita spending on recreation nearly quadrupled in the last three decades. Leisure and recreation are even important enough to have become an academic subject: 350 colleges and universities offer degree programs in it.

The explosion of leisure spending and activities confirms the addition of more free time to our lives. If we hadn't reduced our hours of work, we couldn't spend as much time and money as we do on entertainment and recreation. Americans may find themselves pressed for time, but it's not because we're working harder than we used to. We're busy having fun. . . .

Convenience and Variety

By introducing industrial efficiency to his factories, Henry Ford brought the automobile within the reach of an emerging middle class. The miracle of mass production delivered the goods but didn't adapt easily, so all Model T's looked alike. Ford's attitude can be summed up in what he reputedly said about the car's paint: "The consumer can have any color he wants, as long as its black." Ford's company still makes black cars for drivers who want them, but it now offers a rainbow of colors: red, green, aquamarine, white, silver, purple.

The U.S. marketplace teems with variety. Just since the early 1970s, there's been an explosion of choice: The number of car models is up from 140 to 239, soft drinks from 50 to more than 450, toothpaste brands from four to 35, over-the-counter pain relievers from two to 41.

The market offers 7,563 prescription drugs, 3,000 beers, 340 kinds of breakfast cereal, 50 brands of bottled water. Plain milk sits on the supermarket shelf beside skim milk, 0.5-percent-fat milk, 1-percent-fat milk, 2-percent-fat milk, lactose-reduced milk, hormone-free milk, chocolate milk, buttermilk, and milk with a shelf life of six months. Not long ago, the typical TV viewer had access to little more than NBC, CBS, ABC, and PBS. Today, more than 400 channels target virtually every consumer interest—science, history, women's issues, Congress, travel, animals, foreign news, and more.

Convenience and variety aren't trivial extravagances. They're a wealthy, sophisticated society's way of improving consumers' lot.

Like variety, convenience has emerged as a hallmark of our times. Companies compete for business by putting their products and services within easy reach of their customers.

In 1970 the nation's lone automated teller machine was at the main office of the Chemical Bank in New York. Now ATMs are ubiquitous—not just at banks but at supermarkets, service stations, workplaces, sports facilities, and airports. All told, 273,000 machines offer access to cash 24 hours a day.

Remote controls are proliferating, the newest models incorporating voice-activated technology. Computers and digital devices go with us everywhere. A cell phone is no longer a pricey luxury: The average bill fell from $150 a month in 1988 to $45 in 2001 in constant dollars. No wonder 135 million Americans now own mobile telephones. The number will continue to rise as prices continue to decline and more of us seek the peace of mind and convenience that come with communications in the pocket or purse.

Convenience stores are in nearly every neighborhood. Just one firm, industry leader 7-Eleven, has increased its locations from 3,734 in 1970 to 21,142 today. The Internet may be the ultimate convenience store, bringing shopping into the home. We're buying music, clothing, software, shoes, toys, flowers, and other products with a click of the mouse. Last year [2001], a third of all computers and a fifth of all peripherals were sold online. Thirty-three million buyers ordered books on the Internet, accounting for $1 of every $8 spent in that category.

Convenience and variety aren't trivial extravagances. They're a wealthy, sophisticated society's way of improving consumers' lot. The more choices, the easier access to goods and services the better. A wide selection of goods and services increases the chance that each of us will find, somewhere among all the shelves, showrooms, and Web sites, products that meet our requirements. Convenience allows us to economize on the valuable commodity of time, getting what we want more quickly and easily. . . .

Beyond Statistics

The statistics that measure our economy are reasonably good at counting the value of the cars, clothing, food, sports gear, jewelry, and other goods and services we buy. When we choose an additional hour off over additional income, though, GDP shrinks with the loss of the hour's income and output. We don't count leisure as an economic benefit because we haven't assigned a dollar value to it, even though we opt for time off because it improves our lives.

When it comes to many aspects of a balanced life, our economic barometers come up short. Safety and security are all about preventing bad things from happening. Increased spending on highway safety registers in GDP, but we don't track how much better off we are because of the accidents, injuries, and deaths we avoid. If investing in prevention works, it can actually reduce total output, at least the way we measure it, because less money is spent treating the sick and injured, repairing damage, and replacing lost property.

Our ability to choose a balanced life is one of the market's most important success stories.

Variety makes products more valuable by giving us the designs, colors, and features that fit our preferences, but the statistics count everything as plain vanilla. How conveniently our wants and needs are fulfilled doesn't matter to GDP. A cleaner environment makes for a better country, but it may come at the cost of economic growth.

Inflation-adjusted GDP figures indicate economic growth at an annual average of 3 percent during the last two decades. GDP may be entirely accurate as a tally of how much our farms, factories, and offices produce, but it's increasingly inadequate as a measure of how well the economy provides us with what we want. Our ability to choose a balanced life is one of the market's most important success stories.

Some may argue that it isn't the market that makes a balanced life possible. They might concede that our economy produces abundant goods and services, but they credit government agencies, with their regulations, and unions and pressure groups, with their advocacy, for everything else. History tells us government and advocates play their roles, but they aren't the ultimate source of progress. They don't foot the bill for the choices we make to gain a balanced life. Whatever we want must be paid for, and money ultimately comes from the economy.

Companies improve working conditions because they can afford to, not simply because workers, unions, or government agencies demand it. The dismal work environments in now-defunct socialist nations—all supposedly designed to benefit the worker and eradicate the capitalist—provide a powerful testament to the fact that good intentions are hollow without the ability to pay.

The main role of collective action has been to act as a voice for what we want. Environmental groups formed as the result of our desire for cleaner air and water. When we take our preferences for leisure and better working conditions to unions or elected officials, they help create consensus among employees and lower the cost of communicating these desires to employers.

In the long run, we cannot afford any component of a balanced life—be it consumption, leisure, easier workdays, safety and security, variety and convenience, or environmental cleanup—that we don't earn by becoming more productive. When counting our blessings, we should first thank the economic system. Not federal agencies, not advocacy groups, not unions.

Our quest for a balanced life will never end. The U.S. economy, now recovering from its first recession in a decade [August 2002], will make our society wealthier in the years ahead. We'll take some of our gains in goods and services, but we will also continue to satisfy our desires for the less tangible aspects of life.

Simplicity Offers a Healthy Alternative to Materialism

Wendy Priesnitz

Wendy Priesnitz is an author, journalist, poet, and public speaker. She is also the co-owner of Life Media, an organization that publishes Natural Life *and* Life Learning.

Simplicity offers an alternative to the busy, material-filled lives that many Americans lead. Many people accumulate possessions they rarely use, filling their living spaces with clutter. Simplicity allows one to reduce clutter while also changing habits that lead to clutter; simplicity offers options, such as borrowing or renting instead of buying. Otherwise, possessions become a trap, forcing Americans to work longer hours to acquire items they have no need for.

Simplicity is becoming a 21st century buzzword, a pursuit that is being promoted as a cure for everything from the housework blues and global warming to spiritual malaise.

But there is no mystery to or difficulty about the concept. Simplifying your life is about gaining control of your life—creating more time, on the job and at home, to do the things you want to do. It's also about gaining control of the impact your life makes on the planet.

Surveys show that more and more people feel that they aren't spending their time on things they enjoy. One poll found that 65 percent of people spend their leisure time doing things they'd prefer not to do. And many of these people are asking what's the point of leading a "full life" if you don't have the time and energy to enjoy it, or if it's degrading the environment or other people's quality of life?

Simple living is about streamlining your life so you have time for the people and things you love. It means lightening your load, digging out from under your piles of clutter, as well as the debt and over-committed time required to pay for the stuff that makes up that clutter.

Our Cluttered Lives

Everything you own costs you something, no matter how much or little you originally paid for it. Aside from the cost of acquisition, there are costs associated with a space to store your stuff, the energy to transport it, and your attention to deal with it.

By having only the items that you need, you'll gain a significant cost savings by avoiding the money, space, and energy costs of clutter. If the opportunity to rediscover the richness of daily life doesn't make you want to start cleaning out closets, consider the economy. Cutting back on spending on material goods and learning how to live well on less can be a sort of insurance policy in the face of an uncertain economy with the threat of job loss or falling wages.

I learned to live with fewer belongings a decade or so ago when my husband and I lived in another part of the world for a year and a half. Virtually all of our possessions went into storage (after we purged quite a bit in order not to pay for storing things we didn't need). After a few months away, I started to forget exactly what we owned, let alone miss it. When we finally returned home, we got rid of a lot more stuff, and left some of it in boxes for months after moving into our new home.

But once you're hooked on having lots of possessions, simplifying what you have can seem overwhelming. Begin the process in one small part of your home, such as a closet or a corner of the basement or attic. Examine each item you own and ask yourself if you really need it.

Simplifying your life is about gaining control of your life—creating more time, on the job and at home, to do the things you want to do.

Ask yourself these three questions about each item: Have I used this item recently? Will this item help me attain my life goals? Do I need to own this item or can I rent or borrow it? (Note that sentimental keepsakes you can't bear to part with such as family photo albums or antique heirlooms, or beautiful pieces of art that bring joy to your life could fall under the second question, since they can fulfill an important emotional function along life's path; just don't fall into the trap of keeping everything under the rationalization of nostalgia!) My rule of thumb is that if I haven't used or looked at it in six months, I don't need or want it.

Other criteria to help you decide whether or not to pitch or save involves how you use the item in question. Does it help you be more active, self-reliant, creative and social? Or does it promote passivity, dependence and alienation?

Sort things into three piles: those you want to keep; those you want to give away, sell or recycle; and those suited only for the garbage (and that shouldn't be very big, should it!). You might also want a pile labeled "not sure." Wait a few weeks and go through that pile again; you might feel less attached to these items the second time around or you might decide some of them are too precious to get rid of.

Pay special attention to things that are useful, but not in the quantity you have accumulated. Examples from my home are five saucepans and four frying pans; at least 100 pens; four radios (two of which don't work); innumerable clocks and watches; eight pairs of shoes; four winter coats . . . you get the idea.

Changing Spending Habits

Once you have simplified your possessions, examine ways not to reacquire them. If you thought you needed a bigger house, an addition to your garage, more shelves in the basement, or a remodeled kitchen with more cupboards, maybe having less stuff will eliminate that need.

If you are serious about simpler living, you'll likely have to change your shopping style. Avoid compulsive buying at all costs. One technique is to write down the name of an item that you think you simply must have, then wait for a month. If you still want or need it at that time, go ahead and buy it. You may find that you won't be able to remember why you were so excited about the item in the first place!

Keep in mind that simple living is not about austerity or frugality (although those traits can be important to some people). It's about thoughtfulness and awareness, about not using more resources than you need to, about having the time to do what is really important to you.

If you truly need to acquire something, consider buying used. If buying new, look for quality and durability, as well as standard, simple technology. Avoid the latest fads, and shun equipment that locks you into expensive or hard-to-find replacement parts. Buy compatible items in terms of style and color (my wardrobe is all one color for this reason).

If you are serious about simpler living, you'll likely have to change your shopping style.

For most families, a second car is an unnecessary luxury— one which guzzles money, time and natural resources, in addition to contributing to global warming. If you live in the city, consider getting by with no car at all. Use public transit and pedal power. For much less than the cost of buying and maintaining a car, you can rent a vehicle when you need one, and it will be suited to the task at hand. Or join one of the many car sharing co-ops that are being formed in urban areas.

The borrow or rent principle works for other things too. Do you have to own every book you read, or could you borrow them from the library? Do you need a fully stocked home workshop, or could you rent what you need? Or consider sharing ownership of big items like a lawnmower or mulcher with neighbors; that's not only a great way to minimize possessions but an effective way of building community.

When you're so busy living your life, paying for and managing your possessions, it becomes impossible to imagine anything different. But once you take some time to get rid of possessions that you don't use but that take up space, you will probably start thinking about simplifying other aspects of your life too—moving into a smaller home, simplifying your social life, your volunteer schedule, your finances and eventually your career.

Our lives can be cluttered by possessions that are no longer meaningful. It can also be cluttered by social activities that are attended simply to be polite or out of duty, relationships that no longer work, or household and other duties that have lost meaning or purpose in our lives.

4

Luxury Spending Spurs a Healthy Desire in Self-Improvement

James B. Twitchell

James B. Twitchell teaches at the University of Florida and has written a number of books, including Living It Up: Our Love Affair with Luxury.

Once, the consumption of luxury goods was reserved for the wealthy; now, consuming luxury items has become a way of life for most Americans. Over time, Americans have experienced "luxury creep," as manufactures offer new premium brands of familiar products. In the process, luxury has become more democratic, available to everyone save the poorest fifth of the population. While it is unfortunate that a number of people are left out of the new economy, the desire for luxury may actually improve economic life for many people. The promise of affluence actually seems to motivate many Americans to contribute to the economy. Also, a world in which people are defined by the items they purchase is preferable to one in which they are defined by the color of their skin or their gender.

If you want to understand material culture at the beginning of the 21st century, you must understand the overwhelming importance of unnecessary material. If you are looking for the one unambiguous result of modern capitalism, of the industrial revolution, and of marketing, here it is. In the way we live now, you are not what you make. You are what you consume. And most of what you consume is totally unnecessary yet remarkably well made.

The most interesting of those superfluous objects belong in a socially constructed and ever-shifting class called luxury. Consuming those objects, objects as rich in meaning as they are low in utility, causes lots of happiness and distress. As well they should. For one can make the argument that until all necessities are had by all members of a community, no one should have luxury. More complex still is that, since the 1980s, the bulk consumers of luxury have not been the wealthy but the middle class, your next-door neighbors and their kids. And this is happening not just in the West but in many parts of the world.

When I was growing up in the middle class of the 1950s, luxury objects were lightly tainted with shame. You had to be a little cautious if you drove a Cadillac, wore a Rolex, or lived in a house with more than two columns out front. The rich could drip with diamonds, but you should stay dry. Movie stars could drive convertibles; you should keep your top up. If you've got it, don't flaunt it. Remember, the people surrounding you had lived through the Depression, a time that forever lit the bright lines between have-to-have, don't-need-to-have, and have-in-order-to-show-off.

The best definition of this old-style off-limits luxury came to me from my dad. I was just a kid, and it was my first trip to a cafeteria: Morrison's Cafeteria in Pompano Beach, Florida, February 1955. When I got to the desserts, I removed the main course from my tray and loaded up on cake and JELL-O. My dad told me to put all the desserts back but one. I said that wasn't fair. To me the whole idea of cafeteria was to have as much as you want of what you want. My dad said no, that was not the idea of cafeteria. The idea of cafeteria is that you can have just one of many choices.

Luxury Creep

Look around American culture, and you will see how wrong he was. Almost every set of consumables has a dessert at the top. And you can have as much of it as you can get on your tray or as much of it as your credit card will allow. This is true not just for expensive products like town cars and Mc-Mansions but for everyday objects. In bottled water, for instance, there is Evian, advertised as if it were a liquor. In coffee, there's Starbucks; in ice cream, Haagen-Dazs; in sneakers, Nike; in whiskey, Johnnie Walker Blue; in credit cards, American Express Centurian; in wine, Chateau Margaux; in cigars, Arturo Fuente Hemingway; and, well, you know the rest.

Name the category, no matter how mundane, and you'll find a premium or, better yet, a super-premium brand at the top. And having more than you can conceivably use of such objects is not met with opprobrium but with genial acceptance. This pattern persists regardless of class: The average number of branded sneakers for adolescent males? It's 4.8 pairs. And regardless of culture: A favorite consumer product in China? Chanel lipstick dispensers sans lipstick. . . .

The one characteristic of modern luxe is its profound oxymoronic nature. If everyone can have it, is it still luxury? If you want to see the difference that a generation makes in downshifting luxury, just look at how top-of-the-line domestic automobiles are advertised. Compare Cadillac in the early part of the 20th century with Lincoln at the end of the century, and you'll get the idea.

If you want to understand material culture at the beginning of the 21st century, you must understand the overwhelming importance of unneccessary material.

Cadillac's pitch in a 1915 advertisement was that luxury comes at a price and that price includes humility, even mild mortification. You buy this car and you take responsibility for sharing excellence. The true price of luxury is not cheap. In fact, you will be reviled, assailed, and envied. This car is a laurel. Be careful how you wear it. The real headline is not just "The Penalty of Leadership," it is "The Penalty of Luxury."

By contrast, Lincoln's current pitch is pure indulgence: Buy this object and let your lust for comfort run wild. Lincoln is "what a luxury object should be." And after all you've been through, you deserve it. If not to own, then to lease.

Needless to say, as the 20th century faded into oblivion, Cadillac, which had a history of "owning" the luxury category, lost its vaunted place as the best-selling domestic luxury car to Lincoln. The Lincoln division of the Ford Motor Car Company has a single-word advertising motto: "Luxury."

Perhaps the best example of what I call luxury creep, in which a down-market product comes uptown solely on the basis of advertising, is the Buick Century. Buick has had a history of being a car for strivers who have not quite made it. Just look back on Buick advertising in the '60s, and you can see the company's typical reticence. In 1965 Buick advertising carried the tag line, "Wouldn't you really rather have a Buick?," which survived through the 1980s. In 1980 the company added a second theme: "The great American road belongs to Buick." Then in 1986 the McCann-Erickson ad agency positioned Buicks as "premium American motorcars."

Now Buick does have a luxury car, the Park Avenue. But the Century is an underling, now positioned as "a luxury car for everyone." Never mind that the tag line is an oxymoron. The problem is more fundamental. This car is just a standard Buick, which is just a jazzed-up Chevy, which is just a dumbed-down Cadillac, which is just an Oldsmobile, which is just like tons of Fords and Chryslers, as well as most Japanese midrange cars. The only luxury about it is the pretension of saying this is luxurious.

Luxury for Everyone

In the last few years I have spent hours flipping through a new genre of magazine—*The Robb Report, Millionaire, Indulgence, Flaunt, Luxe, Icon, Self: The Best of Everything, Ornament: The Art of Personal Adornment*—as well as standard glossy pulp from Conde Nast like *GQ, Vogue, Vanity Fair*, and, most recently, *Lucky*. I have trolled Rodeo Drive, Worth Avenue, and upper Madison Avenue and traveled to Las Vegas, where I stood agog for hours in the Bellagio and Venetian hotels.

I admit from the start that you could argue that this is not real luxury but a kind of ersatz variety, punk luxe, and maybe you would be correct. My father would have argued that real luxury is characterized not by shine but by patina, that its allure comes from inborn aesthetics, not from glitzy advertising, that it is passed from generation to generation and cannot be bought at the mall, and, most of all, that its consumption is private, not conspicuous. His words for modern luxury would have included gauche, vulgar, nouveau, tasteless, and, most interestingly, offensive.

The one characteristic of modern luxe is its profound oxymoronic nature: If everyone can have it, is it still luxury?

In fact, maybe the rich have only two genuine luxury items left: time and philanthropy. The rest of us are having a go at all their stuff, albeit for a knockoff to be held only a short time. I can't afford a casita on Bermuda, but my timeshare can get it for me at least for a week. I can't own a limo, but I can rent one. If I can't fly on the Concorde, I can upgrade to first class with the miles I "earn" by using my American Express card. I can lease a Lexus.

In a sense luxury objects don't exist anymore as they used to because "real" luxury used to be for the "happy few," and in the world of the jubilant Dow there is no more "happy few." The world that we live in, as [writer] John Seabrook recently argued in *Nobrow: The Marketing of Culture and the Culture of Marketing*, and as [writer] David Brooks explored in *Bobos in Paradise: The New Upper Class and How They Got There*, no longer easily fits into intellectual classes. It now fits into consumption communities. So, for instance, we don't talk about high class, upper middle class, and middle class. Instead we talk about boomers, yuppies, Generation X, echo-boomers, nobrows, bobos (short for bourgeois bohemians), and the rest, who show what they are buying for themselves, not what they do for a living. And that's why each of these groups has its own luxury markers—positional goods, in marketing jargon—to be bought, not made. . . .

Over-the-Top Luxury

I must say that I found most of the luxury objects that I've looked at, from Patek Philippe watches to Porsche Turbos to the men's room of the Bellagio Hotel, to be a little over the top. But I am not so oblivious to the world around me that I can't appreciate how important the new luxury has become. And I can't overlook how high-end consumption promises to do exactly what critics of the stuff have always yearned for, namely, to bring us together, often traumatically. Yes, indeed, the transgenerational poor are excluded, as the bottom fifth of our population has not budged an inch in the luxe explosion. Yet more people than ever are entering the much-vaunted global village because of consumption, not despite it.

In fact, one could argue, as [authors] Dinesh D'Souza, Virginia Postrel, and W. Michael Cox and Richard Alm have recently done, that the aspiration of the poor to get at these unnecessary goods has done more than any social program to motivate some of the disenchanted to become enfranchised. While one may be distressed at seeing a dish antenna atop a ramshackle house or a Caddie out front, the yearning to have superfluous badges of affluence may promise a more lasting peace around the world than any religion or political system has ever delivered. I don't mean to overlook the complexities here.

In fact, maybe the rich have only two genuine luxury items left: time and philanthropy.

This is not a universal phenomenon, as the al Qaeda have wickedly demonstrated. Some of the world's poor are most certainly not becoming better off in absolute or relative terms. I only want to say that, given a choice between being mugged for your sneakers or having your ethnic or religious heritage cleansed, the lust for sneakers may prove a more lasting way to improve the general lot of humanity.

Let's face it. In the world that I grew up in, your religion, your family name, the color of your skin, your language skills, your gender, where you went to school, your accent, and your marriage partner were doing the work that luxury consumption does now. My dad went to Exeter, Williams, and Harvard Med, and he never drove anything fancier than a Plymouth. He never had to. Today I wouldn't go to a doctor who drove a Plymouth. I would figure that if she doesn't drive a Lexus, she is having trouble with her practice.

A Defense of Luxury Spending

So I admit the ugly truth. After spending the last few years trying to understand the pull of the material world, I am far more sympathetic to its blandishments and far more forgiving of its excesses. The democratization of luxury has been the single most important marketing phenomenon of modern times. And it has profound political implications. It may not be as bad as some lifestyle scolds make it out to be. In its own way it is a fair, albeit often wasteful, system, not just of objects but of meaning. Don't get me wrong: It's not that I came to mock and stayed to pray, but I do feel that getting and spending has some actual worth. Nobody checks the number of vowels in your name, or the color of your skin, or whether you knew the difference between like and as when you are buying your Prada parka—that's got to mean something.

Although luxury has become a mallet with which one pounds the taste of others, this misses some essential points. One is that humans are consumers by nature. We are tool users because we like to use what tool using can produce. In other words, tools are not the ends but the means. So too materialism does not crowd out spiritualism; spiritualism is more likely a substitute when objects are scarce. When we have few things, we make the next world luxurious. When we have plenty, we enchant the objects around us.

The democratization of luxury has been the single most important marketing phenomenon of modern times.

Second, consumers are rational. They are often fully aware that they are more interested in consuming aura than objects, sizzle than steak, meaning than material. In fact, if you ask them—as academic critics are usually loath to do—they are quite candid in explaining that the Nike swoosh, the Polo pony, the Guess? label, the DKNY [Donna Karan New York] logo are what they are after. They are not duped by advertising, packaging, branding, fashion, and merchandising. They actively seek and enjoy the status that surrounds the object, especially when they are young.

Third, we need to question the standard argument that consumption of opuluxe almost always leads to disappointment. Admittedly, the circular route from desire to purchase to disappointment to renewed desire is never-ending, but we may follow it because the other route—from melancholy to angst—is worse. In other words, in a world emptied of inherited values, consuming what looks to be overpriced frip-peries may be preferable to consuming nothing.

Finally, we need to rethink the separation between produc-tion and consumption, for they are more alike than separate and occur not at different times and places but simultaneously. Instead of wanting less luxury, we might find that just the op-posite—the paradoxical luxury for all—is a suitable goal of communal aspiration. After all, luxury before all else is a so-cial construction, and understanding its social ramifications may pave the way for a new appreciation of what has become a characteristic contradiction of our time, the necessary con-sumption of the unnecessary.

5

Corporate Marketing Is Responsible for Childrens' Materialism

Jonathan Rowe and Gary Ruskin

Jonathan Rowe is the director of the Tomales Bay Institute, which concentrates on the expansion of possibilities within American politics. Gary Ruskin is the executive director of Commercial Alert, an institution dedicated to limiting commercial culture.

Marketing experts are bypassing parents to reach children at younger ages. By using television and the Internet, and by placing advertisements in public schools, advertisers are often able to bypass parents when promoting their products to children. As a result, unethical marketers are undermining parents' authority and invading children's privacy. While the government cannot be held responsible for raising America's children, it can create a parents' bill of rights, empowering parents to protect their children from unscrupulous advertisers.

Paul Kurnit is the president of KidShop, an advertising firm that specializes in marketing to children, and he has plans for our kids.

"Kid business has become big business," Kurnit says. To make kid business even bigger, he preaches what he calls "surround marketing": saturation advertising that captures kids at every possible moment.

Jonathan Rowe and Gary Ruskin, "The Parents' Bill of Rights: Helping Moms and Dads Fight Commercialism," *Mothering*, January 2003, pp. 28–35. Copyright © 2003 Mothering Magazine. Reproduced by permission.

"You've got to reach kids throughout the day—in school, as they're shopping at the mall, or at the movies," says Carol Herman, a senior vice president at Grey Advertising. "You've got to become part of the fabric of their lives."

This is what parents today are up against—corporate advertisers who seek to entwine themselves with children's lives. By most measures, the advertisers are succeeding. Each week, the typical American child takes in some 38 hours (yes, a full work week) of commercial media, with its endless ads. And that's not counting the ads that commandeer their attention from billboards and the Internet, the omnipresent brand logos, and the advertising that increasingly fills the schools.

The merchandise pushers have invaded the commons of childhood, the free open spaces of imagination and play, and turned them into a free-fire zone of commercial importuning. In some quarters, this appalling situation is seen as success. "There have never been more ways in the culture to support marketing towards kids," enthuses *Kidscreen*, a publication for ad firms and corporations that target kids. That there's a market for such a publication is revealing.

The merchandise pushers have invaded the commons of childhood, the free open spaces of imagination and play, and turned them into a free-fire zone of commercial importuning.

Corporate advertisers have contrived to wedge themselves into the space between parents and their children. They enlist the best psychologists and market researchers money can buy to lure kids to products and values many of us don't approve of and even abhor. Parents find themselves in a grim daily battle to keep these forces at bay.

On their own, parents cannot contend with the nation's largest corporations and their weapons of mass childhood seduction. It's time Washington stood up for parents. It's time politicians recognized that raising children is the most important task of our society.

Television's Marketing Revolution

Not that long ago, parents actually had control over the front doors of their homes. Sure, a kid might hide a racy magazine under the mattress, but little came into the house without the parents' okay. Even outside the home and school, for adults to approach kids with the thought of influencing them was considered an antisocial act, and offenders could be put in jail.

The invention of electronic media changed all that. The history of the last century, in fact, could be written as the story of how marketers contrived to bypass parents and speak directly to impressionable children. The front door became a permeable membrane, admitting the advertising industry to its promised land. Children are "natural and enthusiastic buyers," a child psychologist wrote in the 1938 book *Reaching Juvenile Markets.* For advertisers, he went on, there was a "tremendous sales potential."

On their own, parents cannot contend with the nation's largest corporations and their weapons of mass childhood seduction.

Psychologists, who are supposed to help children, were now employed to help ensnare them. No longer were such adults considered predators; because they wore suits, sat in offices, and operated at a distance through the media, they were respectable executives and even "pioneers." In the 1930s, the medium was radio; sponsors of children's shows included Ralston cereal and Ovaltine—products that parents actually might have wanted their kids to have—and the ads themselves seem almost tame by today's standards. The young ear is not as impressionable as the eye, and advertisers were still concerned that Mom or Dad might be listening.

Then came television and the beginning of the modern era in the assault on kids. Television is inferior to radio as a storytelling medium; radio engages the imagination, while television numbs it. But as an advertising medium, television is unsurpassed. Children want what they see, and with television, advertisers could offer an endless parade of things to want. After Welch's grape juice became a sponsor of *The Howdy Doody Show* in the 1950s, sales of grape juice to families with young children increased almost five-fold.

With television, moreover, the ads were not just between the shows. They could be in the shows as well. The Disney Corporation created a series about Davy Crockett, starring the actor Fess Parker in a coonskin cap. In short order, kids throughout the country were nagging their parents for the mock coonskin cape that coincidentally began to appear in stores. Crockett gear became a $300 million business—roughly $2 billion in today's dollars.

Increasingly, advertisers had children to themselves. Few parents sat through *The Mickey Mouse Club* or the Saturday-morning cartoon shows. Even shows for general audiences held untapped possibilities. If kids were the most impressionable audience in the house, why not enlist them as sales agents in regard to everything the family bought? "Eager minds can be molded to want your products!" enthused a firm that produced "education" materials for schools. "Sell these children on your brand name, and they will insist that their parents buy no other."

Undermining Parental Authority

Corporations were literally alienating children from their parents, shifting children's loyalties more toward corporations themselves. Rejection of parental authority became a persistent and embedded theme, even in such seemingly innocuous programs as *Howdy Doody*. Television figures became surrogate parents who pushed consumption at every turn. Dr.

Frances Horwich, the kindly "principal" of *Ding Dong School*, popped vitamins and urged her preschool viewers to tell their mothers to pick the bottle with the pretty red pills at the drugstore.

Perhaps it was not entirely accidental that the generation weaned on such fare would become, a decade later, the "Me Generation" of the 1960s. Advertisers were thinking long-term. "Think of what it can mean to your firm in profits," Clyde Miller wrote in *The Process of Persuasion*, "if you can condition a million or ten million children who will grow into adults trained to buy your products as soldiers who are trained to advance when they hear the trigger words 'Forward, march.'"

Children want what they see, and with television, advertisers could offer an endless parade of things to want.

These developments did not go unnoticed. In his landmark book *The Lonely Crowd*, David Riesman observed that corporations had designed a new role for children, as "consumer trainees." In the process, Riesman said, they had turned traditional values upside down. Earlier in the century, children's publications had promoted such qualities as self-discipline and perseverance. "The comparable media today," he wrote, "train the young for the frontiers of consumption—to tell the difference between Pepsi-Cola and Coca-Cola, as later between Old Golds and Chesterfields." (The latter were popular cigarette brands.)

Some parents did resist. In the 1950s there often were a few kids in the neighborhood who were not allowed to watch TV. But most parents then, as now, were reluctant to deny their kids what their friends had. Moreover, parents themselves were caught up in the commercial euphoria of the postwar years, when a new car or television seemed a just reward for the hardships of the Depression and a world war.

Expanding the Children's Market

Soon the commercial saturation of childhood became the new norm, and people hardly noticed anymore. An entire industry arose to mold young minds to crave products, and to cast parents in the subordinate role of financiers of these fabricated wants. James U. McNeal, a former marketing professor at Texas A&M University, is perhaps the most influential advocate of modern marketing to children. "[T]he consumer embryo begins to develop during the first year of existence," McNeal writes, without a hint of embarrassment or shame. "[C]hildren begin their consumer journey in infancy and certainly deserve consideration as consumers at that time."

It is not comforting to know, as we cuddle our newborns, that there exists an industry of James U. McNeals eager to prod them on to their "consumer journey." Nor is it comforting to know that there are marketing consultants, like Cheryl Idell of Western Initiative Media Worldwide, who advise corporations on how to harness the "nag factor" to increase sales. Idell contends that nagging spurs about a third of family trips to fast-food restaurants and purchases of videos and clothing.

Corporations were literally alienating children from their parents, shifting children's loyalties more toward corporations themselves.

And what about the naggees? In the writings of people like McNeal, parents exist as deep pockets to be siphoned by kids, whose role is to influence purchases. This mentality has become the dominant force with which parents must contend. They encounter it at every turn: They take the kids to a sports event and are barraged by ads. They buy a video for them and find that it is chockablock with "product placements"—brand-name products that are built into the story.

Parents feel the heavy breathing of the marketers even on their littlest ones. *Teletubbies,* for example, is an animated TV show aimed at toddlers as young as one year. The producers portray it as educational. But Marly Brochstein, editor of the *Licensing Letter*, is more candid, calling *Teletubbies* a "major big bucks opportunity." The show has done promotions with Burger King and McDonald's. If that's education, it's not the kind most parents have in mind.

Violating Children's Privacy

The morphing of advertising into life extends even to the schools. Corporations have taken advantage of tight school budgets to turn classrooms and hallway walls into billboards for junk food and sneakers. As for the Internet, it's a marketer's dream, a technology that children roam unsupervised, and one that offers endless opportunities for getting into children's minds. "Kids don't realize they're reading advertisements," says Lloyd Jobe, CEO of Skateboard.com.

Marketers know exactly where to find children, too. The collection of children's personal information, and the invasion of their privacy, have become commonplace. American Student List LLC (www.studentlist.com/lists/main.html), a list broker, sells a list of "20 million names of children ranging in age from 2 to 13," along with their addresses, ages, genders, telephone numbers, and other personal information.

For advertisers, it all has been a bonanza: Market researchers estimate that children ages 4 to 12 influence some $565 billion of their parents' purchasing each year, and McNeal calls children the "superstars in the consumer constellation." For kids, however, the role of consumer "superstars" has meant an epidemic of marketing-related diseases. American kids are fatter than ever, and rates of obesity and type 2 diabetes are soaring. Teenage girls have become obsessed with their bodies, due largely to the images of physical perfection that barrage them from fashion magazines, TV, movies, and ads. More than half of all high school girls say they were on diets during the previous month. Likewise, eating disorders are now the third leading chronic illness among adolescent girls.

Our children are being coached and prodded in the arts of petulance and nagging by those whose sole purpose is to turn them into conduits for their parents' money.

Drinking, too, is a problem. A study done by the National Institute on Media and Family found that the more a beer company spends on advertising, the more likely are seventh- to twelfth-graders to know about that beer—and to drink it. Perhaps not coincidentally, alcohol is a factor in the four main causes of death among young people ages 10 to 24: car crashes, other accidents, homicide, and suicide.

The merchants of death are adept at using marketing to undermine the good influence of parents. Tobacco marketing is especially successful at counteracting parents who encourage their children not to smoke. Each day, another 3,000 children start to smoke; the lives of roughly a third of them will be shortened by smoking-related illnesses.

Marketing Creates Family Conflicts

Added to all this is the production of misery and dissension in the home. Our children are being coached and prodded in the arts of petulance and nagging by those whose sole purpose is to turn them into conduits for their parents' money. As anthropologist Jutes Henry once noted, advertising has become an "insolent usurper of parental function, degrading parents to mere intermediaries between children and the market."

A survey by the Merck Family Fund found that 86 percent of Americans think that young people today are "too focused on buying and consuming things." *Business Week*, no enemy of corporate America, perhaps put it best: "Instead of transmitting a sense of who we are and what we hold important, today's marketing-driven culture is instilling in [children] a sense that little exists without a sales pitch attached and that self-worth is something you buy at a shopping mall."

You might think our representatives in Washington would show some concern, but politicians in both major parties seem reluctant to stand up to commercial predators. Back in the late 1970s, for example, the Federal Trade Commission (FTC) proposed an end to advertising to children too young to grasp that ads aren't necessarily true. In response, Congress stripped the FTC of any authority to enact rules against advertisers who take advantage of the vulnerabilities of impressionable youth. J. Howard Beales III, the FTC's chief of consumer protection in the current administration, is an economist perhaps best known for his scholarly defense of R.J. Reynolds and its infamous "Joe Camel" advertising campaign. David Scheffman, the new head of the FTC's bureau of economics, also worked for the tobacco industry.

Parents deserve a little more respect. Their job is hard enough without the marketing culture treating them as cannon fodder. The technology of seduction has increased tremendously in sophistication and reach, and corporate seducers have gained new legal rights. Yet the means for parents to contend with these intrusions, and to talk back to the intruders, have scarcely grown at all. In many respects, they have diminished.

The time has come to right the balance. The government can't do parents' jobs for them, but it certainly can give them the legal rights they need to stand up effectively to corporations that target their kids. Parents should not be second-class citizens. They should not feel under siege by a culture designed to shake them down for money, and to usurp the function of instilling values in their kids.

6

Parents Are Responsible for Children's Embrace of Consumer Culture

James J. Farrell

James J. Farrell is a professor of history at St. Olaf College in Minnesota and the author of One Nation Under Goods: Malls and the Seduction of American Shopping.

While many Americans wear T-shirts that state they were "born to shop," the reality is quite different. Children, in fact, learn to shop by watching their parents. As parents allow children to accompany them to the grocery store and the mall, they are teaching their children how to become consumers. By dressing a child in a particular style clothing, parents teach children the importance of brand names and status within the consumer culture. Other tools, like an allowance, socialize children in money management. Allowances and other financial rewards also underline parents' complicity in consumer socialization: Parents want their children to become consumers.

At many malls, you can find a t-shirt or a bumper sticker bearing the cheerful message "Born to Shop," a message that, on reflection, seems demonstrably false. Indeed, despite its omnipresence in American society, shopping is neither a natural nor instinctual act. In the Bible, American culture's main religious account of creation, there's not much evidence that people were created to shop. Even on the seventh day, when God rested, He didn't go shopping with his human creatures. In Genesis, of course, after the Fall, Adam and Eve clothed themselves because they were ashamed. But there's no textual evidence that they shopped for their apparel.

And there's little scientific evidence for the proposition that people are genetically wired for consumerism. Indeed, anybody who has seen a newborn baby can testify that they're not yet equipped for shopping. They have desires, an essential element of shopping, but they're not ready for malls of America. Nor is there much historical evidence that people are congenital shoppers. Although many Americans consider shopping almost a birthright, history shows that people lived fully human lives for thousands of years without shopping.

"Born to Shop" t-shirts to the contrary, shopping is a social construction, and we *learn* to shop as we learn to speak and write and dine and drive. As Barbara Kingsolver suggests, "Human young are not born with the knowledge that wearing somebody's name in huge letters on a T-shirt is a thrilling privilege for which they should pay eighty dollars. It takes several years of careful instruction to arrive at that piece of logic." The instruction begins early: the average American child makes a first trip to a mall at two months of age. By two years, American kids can name a product. By four, they can evaluate a product, and at six they've internalized the idea that "better brands cost more." At the relatively late age of eleven, they begin to understand that some claims are misleading. In this culture, growing up means growing to be shoppers.

'Born to Shop' t-shirts to the contrary, shopping is a social construction, and we learn to shop as we learn to speak and write and dine and drive.

Our kids need this education, because few American malls provide detailed instructions for shopping. For the most part, malls are merely warehouses—huge spaces filled with stuff displayed for our delectation. When you march into the mall from the parking lot, there's no sign with the rules or etiquette of shopping. There's precious little information about items at the mall. Clothes are piled on tables, or hang from racks, and signs indicate only the brand name or the price. Occasionally a sign screams "Sale" or "Clearance," but generally speaking, the mall keeps its secrets. It gives us precious little information about the process of shopping. Malls presume that we already know. And we do. But *how* do we know? How do we learn to shop?

Before we actually go to the mall on our own, we learn how to act when we're there. Called "consumer socialization," this learning is basically the preparatory course for malls of America. We learn where to park and where to enter. We learn about longing and desire, about the difference between window shopping and shoplifting. We learn what to say when the salesperson asks, "May I help you?" We learn about money and credit cards, and how to make a transaction at the cash register. In short, we learn the "common sense" of shopping. Einstein said that "common sense is the collection of prejudices acquired by age eighteen," and most of us have acquired our consumer's common sense by that age. . . .

Bringing Up Baby

Even before our babies come home from the hospital, we've begun the process of teaching them how to consume. We've often prepared a nursery, for example, by decorating a room or corner with new paint or wallpaper, a crib and changing table, a mobile and assorted plush toys. We don't do these things for the baby, who isn't yet looking at things with a critical consumer's eye, we do them to tell our friends and relatives how we feel about children and about the child's relationship to the world of goods. The baby just got home and already she has a life-style. She's too young to appreciate it, but she'll breathe it in like air. The nursery nurses a child's sense of the meaning of goods.

It's a parent's responsibility to feed and clothe and shelter children, and we do this—as parents always have—in the world of goods. Most American parents fulfill these parental responsibilities in the world of branded consumer commodities. We have to decide between Pampers and Huggies, Cheerios and Frosted Flakes, Gymboree and Baby Gap. We choose the colonial house over the contemporary home, the Chevrolet over the Ford, the private over the public school. In raising children responsibly, we teach them to respond to the world of consumer culture. Because we love our kids, we provide things for them to consume. And in the process, we teach them that shopping and brands matter to people who matter.

The things we buy our kids are, in many ways, an expression of our hopes and fears for them. We buy them clothes that fit them and help them fit in. We buy books and videos and toys and computers to stimulate their imagination and teach them about the world. We buy food and drink to nourish them (and candy and ice cream to please them). We buy museum memberships and souvenirs to help them make cultural attachments. We buy bicycles and sporting goods that enable them to develop skills of play and teamwork. Often, we make substantial sacrifices to make these purchases. In America, we love our children by shopping for them.

Even before our babies come home from the hospital, we've begun the process of teaching them how to consume.

Kids are also a way we express our own taste and status. Increasingly, we clothe middle-class children not just in garments, but in assumptions about the cachet of the clothes. A baby doesn't care if it's dressed in Baby Gap, but many parents do. So many American merchandisers, and many fashion designers, have extended their product lines to include clothes for kids. Tommy Hilfiger even licenses a designer-dressed doll that's sold at FAO Schwarz. Ralph Lauren markets clothes for girls at a web site called ralphlaurengirls.com. The name implies that the kids may own the clothes but Ralph Lauren owns the girls. When we dress our children in such fashions, we make them into designer kids—kids designed in part by professional fashion designers and kids designed to be designer-conscious.

By our own purchases and participation in the commercial economy, we teach kids a set of assumptions about home as the preeminent site of consumption. We pass on our conception of "home, sweet home"—our belief that the home should be a haven in a heartless world and that it's a sweet haven because it's where we get to enjoy the stuff we've earned in the workplace. But we generally don't teach kids that the home, which is our respite from the world, rests on the world's foundation. We don't show them how our home, through its consumption patterns, is interconnected with hundreds of other homes throughout the world.

Home Schooling (in Consumption)

From birth we teach our children how to be consumers. We teach them that in our culture, everything is possessed, everything belongs to someone. We teach our kids the concepts of ownership and property by showing them how to say "Mine!" and we teach them how to make things "Mine!" by buying them. As journalist Constantine Von Hoffman suggests, "An honest look reveals us as happy and willing participants in indoctrinating our child in consumerism." We try to teach our children family values, but we often forget that our families *value* commercial goods, and that kids know it. To most American children, consumption *is* a family value.

Kids learn the pleasures of consumption before they learn any of its costs. As dependents of adults, they can be independent of the responsibilities of consumption. So kids' first encounters with the culture of consumption give them a taste of gratification without any aftertaste. They are oblivious to the consequences of consumption, and, as protective parents, we try to maintain that oblivion as long as possible. Many Americans never figure out the consequences of consumption. Having learned to think narrowly about the costs and benefits of consumerism, we maintain our *my* opia into adulthood and middle age.

From birth we teach our children how to be consumers. We teach them that in our culture, everything is possessed, everything belongs to someone.

As soon as kids can count, we teach them simple mathematics by teaching them to count money. A nickel is five pennies, a dime is two nickels, a quarter is two dimes and a nickel, and so on. We also teach them addition and subtraction by offering retail story problems: if apples are two for a quarter, and you have a dollar, how many apples can you buy (assuming, of course, that there's no sales tax on food)? Both at home and at school, we teach our kids how to make change, as if they might someday work at the mall. By second grade, we've generally succeeded: most American children know the value of coins and bills and how to use money in the marketplace. The manifest function of such teaching is a mastery of numbers and mathematical operations, but the latent function is the naturalization of money and market exchange. By teaching kids to make change, therefore, we teach them not to make any significant changes in our market economy.

Later, allowances and other sources of income allow kids to participate as consumers in the commercial economy. In a country with strict child labor laws, American children usually make money only with parental consent. Between the ages of four and twelve, they make about fifteen dollars a week, and they spend two-thirds of it immediately. [Marketing expert] James McNeal suggests that the dramatic increase in children's income in the last twenty years shows that "parents want their children—expect their children—to be practicing consumers." Most of us understand an allowance as training in money management, an essential skill for a maturing American. We hope that kids will learn to save their money and, in some cases, make contributions to churches and charities. But an allowance also introduces children to autonomous consumption, and it usually privileges individual choices over group choices.

When money is given to children as a payment for work performed, for household chores or for academic grades, it also teaches children responsibility, even as it frees parents to work longer hours. Kids now perform about 10 percent of household work in America, and they make about $5 billion a year performing housework. Payment for that work introduces children to wage labor, and to the pattern of accepting extrinsic rewards for their work. It also teaches children that consumption is the standard reward for productive activity.

Family Shopping Trips

The rituals of family life also inevitably immerse children in the commercial economy. Some families read the Sunday paper together in preparation for a weekly shopping excursion. Many of us go out to eat on special occasions. We teach kids how to participate in the gift rituals of American life, those occasions when we define relationships with meaningful things. We celebrate birthdays, for example, by giving gifts— often purchased in America's malls. As kids invite friends to their birthday parties, and, even more important, when they go to birthday parties, they learn about the commodification of care. They learn how to express their feelings for friends by buying them "cool" toys or fashionable clothes. They know that, in general, the more expensive the gift, the better. Within the family, kids know that they can make gifts for their parents and siblings up to a certain age. But after that, they're often expected to buy manufactured goods to express their personal feelings.

Americans also use the religious festival of Christmas to deepen our children's home schooling in consumption. During the Christmas season, we may or may not attend religious observances, but we almost certainly will be in attendance at the mall. During the Christmas season, we teach our children how to express their own desires by making lists and communicating them to Santa Claus, either in person or by mail. We teach them to express affection, or at least to feign affection, by buying appropriate gifts for the special people in their lives. We teach them the rules of American gift giving. We show them how social relationships can be reinforced by the exchange of things. . . . Christmas, perhaps the preeminent public ritual of American life, is suffused with consumption.

Americans also use the religious festival of Christmas to deepen our children's home schooling in consumption.

Some of us mentor our children carefully in the practices of consumption. We talk to them about purchases and prices. We teach them how to clip coupons, how to wait for a sale, how to determine the quality of products. We pass our shopping patterns, retail preferences, and brand loyalties from generation to generation, making consumption both familiar and familial. Some of us read advice books to help us teach our children well. In *Piggy Bank to Credit Card: Teach Your Child the Financial Facts of Life*, for example, Linda Barbanel offers a detailed road map to consumer education for kids. But most American parents "appear to have few educational goals in mind and make limited attempts to teach consumer skills." In general, we leave consumption to the informal curriculum of life. We seem to expect children to learn consumption on their own. Of course, to a great degree, they do.

7

Consumerism Harms the Environment

S.M. John Kennedy

S.M. John Kennedy is the assistant headmaster at St. Xavier's College in India. He also conducts seminars on eco-awareness.

The world is currently facing an environmental crisis because of unchecked consumerism. This selfish overexploitation of natural resources has threatened numerous plant and animal species with extinction. Capitalist countries like the United States have been the biggest culprits, using 25 percent of the world's energy and exploiting Third World economies. If these tendencies remain unchecked, the pollution caused by consumerism threatens both the air and water that humans need to sustain life.

Science has developed by leaps and bounds. The entire world has become one global village through the network of communication. New inventions have smoothened modern life. *Yet, despite these stupendous developments, one is tempted to ask whether the quality of life has really been enhanced. Life is in greater peril now.* The entire universe has become a dumping ground for noxious gases and toxic elements. More than ever, life is threatened with immediate collapse due to the environmental crisis. Human beings have altered everything in nature to suit their conveniences and luxuries and thus their very survival is now endangered. Can one species plunder and loot the great but limited wealth of the earth?

S.M. John Kennedy, "Consumerism Is a Planetary Sin," *Integral Liberation*, March 2005. Reproduced by permission.

Today's Ecological Crisis

Biodiversity refers to three elements: the variety of species; the variety within the species, for no two individuals are the same; and the variety of the ecosystems on which these species are subsisting. It is estimated that there are about 30 million different species of plants and animals on this earth. But only 10,75,850 animal species and 3,500,000 plant species have so far been discovered and scientifically explained. Humans, being only one among these species, should neither completely control nor overexploit the resources of the earth. They have to acknowledge the basic right of the other species to share the wealth of the earth. Instead, they not only deny them their rightful due but also threaten them with extinction.

It is estimated that, at the present rate of extinction, about 25% of our biological wealth will have permanently disappeared within the next 30 years. Besides, our planet is slowly becoming inhospitable for any living organism. According to the Red Data book by the UNEP [United Nations Environmental Programme], 183 species of fishes, 138 species of amphibians and reptiles, 400 species of birds, 305 species of mammals and 25,000 species of plants are threatened with extinction. The extinction takes place due to various reasons: habitat destruction, over-exploitation, introduction of alien and exotic species, competition for food with humans and illegal poaching. *In fact, the whole environment is being destabilised today.*

Human beings have altered everything in nature to suit their conveniences and luxuries and thus their very survival is now endangered.

Global problems such as climate change, destruction of forests, over-exploitation and annihilation of biodiversity, desertification, ozone hole, and over-utilisation and contamination of water sources, are causing irreversible damages to the biosphere and human life. The greed for wealth and lust for material prosperity have reduced our billions-year-old 'mother earth' into a rubbish rubble.

Humans have indeed brought our planet to the edge of a suicidal cliff. *For the first time in history, we seem capable of 'ecocide', the destruction of the entire ecology. The crisis of the eco-system reflects the deep crisis of human society—its economy, ethos and set of values.* The ecological crisis has its roots in our vision of the whole of creation, our priorities and value-system. All of this highlights the religio-moral dimensions of the crisis. *Our response must therefore find a social expression which impinges on both the structures and values of our society.* One such structure is the present economic system.

Capitalism and Environmental Degradation

With capitalism peaked the environmental crisis. The worst enemies of the environment are the capitalist countries. The mechanistic worldview developed by scholars like John Locke, Francis Bacon and René Descartes resulted in the onslaught of industrialisation. The only aim of capitalism is profit at all costs. The natural resources fulfilling the basic needs of the vast majority were diverted to create luxuries for a few. *This led to a lopsided development where a few enjoy all the earth's resources, while the vast majority suffer from poverty, deprivation and malnutrition.*

The greed for wealth and lust for material prosperity have reduced our billions-year-old 'mother earth' into a rubbish rubble.

In this wounded and divided world, the earth is deprived of its rightful existence and role in the cosmos. The myth of 'progress' is projected as the central value, measured by society's performance as quantified in terms of gross national product, net national product, 'growth' of the economy, etc. This confuses superficial 'having' with 'being'. . . .

About 5% of the world's population in America uses 25% of the energy! One American spends as much as 8,150 Indians in terms of natural resources and waste generation. *This distribution/utilisation of the world's resources, which involves a downright deprivation and exploitation of the vast majority, is a planetary sin.* It is against natural justice. For every human and other organism has a right to share in the resources of the earth and survive.

Capitalism, actively promoted through globalisation, has resulted in consumerism by which luxuries are converted into basic needs, without which life is made to look incomplete and inadequate. The quality and dignity of life are believed to be enhanced by the things possessed. Resources meant to fulfill the basic needs of all the organisms are thus diverted to satisfy the created luxuries of a few. The accumulation of such goods is the end-product of consumerism. Advertisements market these luxuries. Globalisation is the vehicle through which consumerism is promoted throughout the world. . . .

Consumerism Is a Planetary Sin

The globalised economy with its craze for lavish and extravagant living is inflicting irreversible/irreparable damages on the environment. Growth and development are being achieved by increasing pollution and waste. The damages caused to the environment by global trade are not usually given serious consideration. The uncontrolled consumption of natural resources has dried up the finite resources of the planet. The drive for mass production leads to the overuse of natural resources and thus endangers the ecological balance. It also cuts down public expenditure, which by and large results in less protection of the environment. Our health and survival depends upon the environment—the air we breathe, the water we drink and the food we eat. But the global trade has no regard for a sustainable economy: it pollutes the air and water and poisons the food.

The technologies associated with globalisation create havoc with the environment. Aeroplanes pollute the air through toxic waste and motor-ships dirty the seas. Forests are being cleared, minerals completely stripped out and fossil fuels over-exploited. Overfishing for global trade has wiped out marine resources. Global wood production has led to the hacking down of 60% of the world forests, which has killed 10,000 tree species. Fertile soils are ruined by erosion and desalinisation. Globalised trade increased the use of transport and the pollution, and contributed to cause a hole in the ozone layer. Every year, nearly 3 million people die from air pollution and 8 million suffer from it.

Growth and development are being achieved by increasing pollution and waste. The damages caused to the environment by global trade are not usually given serious consideration.

Since the emphasis is on global trade instead of local trade, small farmers are being displaced because cheap and subsidised imports undercut agricultural production. Imported food is increasingly preferred to local farm produce. Many farmers are now abandoning farming. In the US, "small farms are disappearing at the rate of 30,000 per year". In India, multinational agribusiness companies now demand that farmers buy genetically modified seeds, forcing them to give up their traditional seeds year after year. The US multinational Rice Tec. has even gained the patent of Basmati rice, grown in India for centuries.

In global production and trade, it is easy to relocate a company to a place where there are less stringent environmental rules. This is why many mega companies have shifted from the North to the South. And they have also sometimes transferred tons of toxic wastes. *The poor and the marginalised do not benefit from globalisation.* Rather, they are exploited in factories and sweat shops all over the world. The rich and the powerful, unfettered by national barriers and rules, pocket the profits of globalisation and consumerism. A trade policy that benefits only a few is undemocratic. *Thus capitalism, globalisation and consumerism are forces of oppression, exploitation and injustice.* Moreover, they deny the right share of the earth's resources to other organisms. *They are a sin against planet earth and all its people, present and future.*

Towards Alternatives

We shall sail together or sink together in the spaceship EARTH. We therefore need to act with the greatest urgency. It is now or never. Here are some steps towards a healthy living.

- *Healthy and cosmocentric (not anthropocentric) thinking, outlook and worldview.* Humans are one among the other species. All are interdependent and interconnected. Look at the planet with the eyes of the still to be born and from the interests of the other organisms.

- Environmental economics where the economy takes into account the environmental concerns. The ecology overrides economics.

- Commercialise and economise the alternate sources of energy.

- Subsistence economy where the economy is oriented and geared towards fulfilling the fundamental needs of the vast majority of the people.

- Respecting the rightful needs of the other species and providing them the needed resources.

- *Sustainable, simple, environment-friendly living.*

8

Environmental Harm Caused by Consumerism Is Overstated

Jack Hollander

Jack Hollander is professor of energy and resources at the University of California at Berkeley and the author of The Real Environmental Crisis: Why Poverty, Not Affluence, Is the Environment's Number One Enemy.

Newspapers and magazines bombard contemporary readers with negative stories of imminent environmental doom. Affluent society, we are told, is responsible for global warming and other environmental problems. But the criticism misses an underlying truth: Only by producing affluence does a society have the resources to maintain a healthy environment. The real threat to the environment is poverty, not affluence, because poor societies, in an attempt to meet basic needs, show little concern for the careful use of resources. Reducing poverty is the key to reducing environmental degradation.

Can you remember a day when you opened your morning newspaper *without* finding a dramatic and disturbing story about some environmental crisis that's either here already or lurks just around the corner? That would be a rare day. On one day the story may be about global warming; on the next it may be about overpopulation or air pollution or resource depletion or species extinction or sea-level rise or nuclear waste or toxic substances in our food and water. Especially jarring is the implication in most of these stories that *you and I are the enemy*—that our affluent lifestyles are chiefly responsible for upsetting nature's balance; polluting our cities, skies, and oceans; and squandering the natural resources that sustain us. Unless we change our thoughtless and wasteful ways, we are reminded, the earth will become a very inhospitable place for ourselves and our progeny.

Such media reportage reflects the pervasive pessimism about the future that has become the hallmark of today's environmental orthodoxy. Its central theme is that the *affluent* society, by its very nature, is the *polluting* society—the richer we become, the more we consume the earth's scarce resources, the more we overcrowd the planet, the more we pollute the earth's precious land, air, and water. The clear implication of this viewpoint is that the earth was a better place before humans were around to despoil it.

Affluence is a key ingredient for ensuring a livable and sustainable environment for the future

---

Some people, even some environmental scientists, genuinely subscribe to this gloomy picture of the earth's future. I do not hold that they are necessarily uninformed, or naive, or unprofessional, or captive to special interests. But they are indeed pessimistic. I am more optimistic about the earth's environmental future, and I believe there is plenty of evidence to support an optimistic, though not cornucopian, view of the environmental future. . . .

In my judgment, people are not the enemy of the environment. Nor is affluence the enemy. Affluence does not inevitably foster environmental degradation. Rather, affluence fosters *environmentalism*. As people become more affluent, most become increasingly sensitive to the health and beauty of their environment. And gaining affluence helps provide the economic means to protect and enhance the environment. Of course, affluence alone does not guarantee a better environment. A sense of social responsibility is also required. Political will is also required. *But affluence is a key ingredient for ensuring a livable and sustainable environment for the future.*

The Real Enemy of the Environment Is Poverty

The real enemy of the environment is *poverty*—the tragedy of billions of the world's inhabitants who face hunger, disease, and ignorance each day of their lives. Poverty is the environmental villain; poor people are its victims. Impoverished people often do plunder their resources, pollute their environment, and overcrowd their habitats. They do these things not out of willful neglect but only out of the need to survive. They are well aware of the environmental amenities that affluent people enjoy, but they also know that for them the journey to a better environment will be long and that their immediate goal must be to escape from the clutches of poverty. They cannot navigate this long journey without assistance— assistance from generous institutions, nations, and individuals and from sincere and effective policies of their own governments.

For the affluent nations to assist people in the developing world is socially responsible and morally right. But from an environmental perspective the issue is more than ethical. It is pragmatic as well, since the environmental self-interests of the affluent would be well served by the eradication of poverty. This idea disturbs those who fear that people emerging from poverty will inevitably become "wasteful" consumers like ourselves and will only exacerbate the globe's environmental damage as they pursue the trappings of the good life. The fear is understandable, but the conclusion is wrong. Without doubt, people tasting affluence will embrace consumerism and become proud owners of property, vehicles, computers, cell phones, and the like. But they will also pursue education, good health, and leisure for themselves and their families. And *they will become environmentalists.*

The essential prerequisites for a sustainable environmental future are a global transition from poverty to affluence, coupled with a transition to freedom and democracy.

Environmentalists are made, not born. In the industrial countries environmentalism arose as a reaction to the negative impacts of early industrialization and economic growth. On the way from subsistence to affluence, people developed a greater sense of social responsibility and had more time and energy to reflect about environmental quality. They had experienced environmental deterioration firsthand, and they demanded improvement. One of the great success stories of the recent half-century is, in fact, the remarkable progress the industrial societies have made, during a period of robust economic growth, in reversing the negative environmental impacts of industrialization. In the United States the air is cleaner and the drinking water purer than at any time in five decades; the food supply is more abundant and safer than ever before; the forested area is the highest in three hundred years; most rivers and lakes are clean again; and, largely because of technological innovation and the information revolution, industry, buildings, and transportation systems are more energy- and resource-efficient than at any time in the past. This is not to say that the resource/environment situation in the United States is near perfect or even totally satisfactory—of course it is not. Much more needs to be done. But undeniably, the improvements have been remarkable. They have come about in a variety of ways—through government regulation, through taxation, through financial incentives, through community actions. Most important, these environmental improvements cannot be credited solely to government, environmental organizations, or lobbyists, though each has played an important role. Rather, they have come about because the majority of citizens in this and every other democratic affluent society demands a clean and livable environment. Does this imply that the affluent have achieved an improved environment in their own lands by exporting their pollution to the lands of the poor? That has rarely been the case. . . .

As the industrial societies continue to make steady progress in reclaiming their environment, they are now laying the foundation for a postindustrial future that is globally sustainable. Some elements of this foundation already exist everywhere— people's technological ingenuity, creativity in finding solutions to emerging problems, political will to get the job done. Other elements of this foundation do not yet exist or are weak. The central argument of this book is that *the essential prerequisites for a sustainable environmental future are a global transition from poverty to affluence, coupled with a transition to freedom and democracy.* . . .

Espousing optimism about the environment does not imply being complacent or sweeping environmental problems under the rug.

My optimism about the environmental future is at odds with the environmental orthodoxy as practiced by most environmental organizations and the media, and especially reflected in the increasing stridency of their doomsday predictions of the environmental future. There is a double irony here. First, so bleak an outlook has arisen during the very period in which the affluent societies have been making their greatest environmental and economic gains; and second, the citizenry in the affluent countries overwhelmingly support a clean environment and are becoming increasingly alienated by the hyperbolic excesses committed in the name of environmentalism. . . .

Optimism, Not Inaction

Please do not misunderstand me. Espousing optimism about the environment does not imply being complacent or sweeping environmental problems under the rug. On the contrary, optimism implies a "can do" attitude that makes success in dealing with such problems more likely. Despair and inaction are more likely to arise from pessimism about the future than from optimism. Nor does environmental optimism equate with denial. Of course, real environmental concerns are still with us. They always have been, and they always will be. As long as humans, imperfect species that we are, live together in this increasingly interdependent global village, there will be problems arising from people's activities and interactions, as well as risks arising from human adventures and technological innovations. The environment is no exception. Although, obviously, not all environmental problems are caused by human activities, humans everywhere bear a collective responsibility to care for this planet as best we can, on the basis of the scientific knowledge we have.

Without question, environmental organizations and the media have played a historically important role in bringing important information about the environment to public attention. They should continue to do so. But performing the role of environmental watchdog does not confer license to exaggerate, mislead, or strike fear in the hearts of a largely supportive public earnestly looking for information and guidance. Scientists, specialist organizations (whether representing environmental or other interests), and the media have a collective responsibility not to cross the line separating truth, however well or poorly known, from self-serving rhetoric. Unfortunately, by exaggerating many environmental problems far out of proportion to the actual or potential threats they may pose to society's future, the purveyors of doomsday rhetoric create a climate of confusion and fear about the environment among a citizenry inadequately equipped with the scientific background needed to calibrate such rhetoric.

With environmental matters, as with most others, informed discussion is the key to effective decision making in a democratic society.

How could people not become fearful about global warming, for example, when they are bombarded incessantly with alarming and simplistic predictions of global catastrophe from climate change that is purportedly caused by human activities? In truth, climate change is a dynamic natural phenomenon that has been occurring ever since the earth was formed millions of years ago, and the extent of human culpability for perturbing this natural system is far from established. Climate science is so extraordinarily complex that not even leading climate scientists profess to understand climate change fully. One thing that climate scientists do understand, however, is that current predictions of future climate are based almost entirely on computer simulations. Although simulations are a widely used tool in science research generally and are essential for meteorologists' short-term weather predictions, they do not provide an adequate basis for the catastrophic generalizations about future climate often made by environmental organizations and the media. In any case, for most of us it is difficult to distinguish between solid empirical evidence and speculation based on highly uncertain computer models.

Environmental exaggeration also emanates on occasion from political leaders. For example, in his book *Earth in the Balance*, former vice president Al Gore states that climate change is "the most serious threat we've ever faced," and "Our insatiable drive to rummage deep beneath the surface of the earth, remove all of the coal, petroleum, and other fossil fuels we can find, then burn them as quickly as they are found—in the process filling the atmosphere with carbon dioxide and other pollutants—is a willful expansion of our dysfunctional civilization into vulnerable parts of the natural world." In contrast to the book's extreme rhetoric, Gore's actual voting record on environmental issues in the Senate was centrist.

With environmental matters, as with most others, informed discussion is the key to effective decision making in a democratic society. Extreme rhetoric serves less to catalyze rational discussion of issues than it does to polarize people's views and create fear and confusion about the environment. Some scientists argue (usually in private) that creating fears about environmental risks is an effective antidote to public apathy and complacency and that the public's environmental fears can take credit for much of their support for environmental actions. I take issue with that view and prefer to believe that a truthfully informed public is more likely than a fearful public to be supportive of meaningful responses. I would place my bets that the wisest public choices about the environment will come about from disciplined presentations by scientists, and others, of research results and from contending interpretations unembellished by exaggerations and doomsday scenarios.

When individuals and the media in the affluent countries characterize as imminent threats such issues as overpopulation, resource exhaustion, and global warming, they cause more than fear: they cause actual harm by diverting people's attention and, more important, their resources from critical global problems that cry out for solution, especially the proliferation of weapons of mass destruction and the world's most formidable and pervasive environmental problem—poverty.

9

Buying Leads to Happiness

Hillary Johnson

Hillary Johnson writes for the Los Angeles Times Magazine *and* Real Simple *and has authored a novel,* Physical Culture, *and a collection of essays,* Super Vixens' Dymaxion Lounge.

Impulse buying may lead to illogical decisions, but nonetheless a psychological value is derived from these purchases. As we make these choices, we are also defining ourselves. Only by purchasing an item we think we want can we be sure if the item truly fits our personality. Even items that fail to be useful are nonetheless beneficial: They bring peace of mind by helping us to define the limits of who we are.

I am an unrepentant impulse buyer. A few weeks ago, while walking past a secondhand store, I stumbled upon an absolutely gargantuan throne-like armchair. It was upholstered in a loud red, white, blue, and gold print featuring eagle crests, portraits of George Washington, and ribbon banners that read "Freedom," "Liberty," and "1776." With its matching ottoman, it took up almost as much floor space as a double bed. It was magnificent, and I immediately recognized it for what it was: the Ugliest Chair in the World. Was this the so-bad-it's-good find of the decade? Quite possibly. My heart thrilled.

My immediate instinct was to swoop in and buy it without even thinking—just because I knew no one would believe my description of it. I was thinking of the first time I saw a John Waters movie and tried to explain it to someone who didn't know what on earth I was talking about. Some things in life just can't be explained—they must be seen.

The chair is by no means the first wayward, inappropriate, or misguided purchase I have made in my life, and I'll readily admit that it will not be the last. I am prone to guilt over a lot of minor things: I feel guilty about forgotten birthdays, late credit-card payments, unreturned phone calls, and the fact that I usually forget to remove my eye makeup before falling into bed. But I am completely over feeling guilty about the spoils of my feckless career as an impulse buyer—the clothes that have hung in my closet for five years with the price tags still on them, the gadgets and home-decor items piled up in the garage.

Over the years, the collection of shame (as my boyfriend calls it, though I feel none) has included everything from hot pink suede boots to a vacation cabin. My closets are full of props and costumes for lives I have somehow never gotten around to living: three cotton sarongs, half-a-dozen cocktail dresses, a Burberry skirt, several pairs of unhemmed dress slacks, and three Brooks Brothers button-down shirts with the hang tags still on them. Crammed onto shelves in the garage are the household items. Among them: dog-grooming clippers, an uninflated exercise ball, a tent, a Cuisinart Mini-Prep, and a pair of rechargeable two-way radios. Most of these items were bought in good faith, and I can't say that the impulses behind purchasing them were wrong. If I groomed my own dog, exercised, spent my weekends camping, threw dinner parties, and had the kind of job—and income—that necessitated the wearing of Burberry and Brooks Brothers, I'd probably be in a lot better shape than I am now.

Buying Peace of Mind

Of course, not all the items are useful or virtuous, even in theory. Don't ask me why I have six hand drums, or three vintage fur coats when I live in suburban Southern California, or why the last time I went into the laundry room I gashed my toe open on a rack of antlers that just happened to be poking out from under the shelf where we keep the detergent.

And then there's that vacation cabin I went in on with friends, possibly the ne plus ultra [highest point] of impulse buys. It wasn't as expensive as it probably sounds, since it had no plumbing, electricity, or direct road access. But even a $20 pair of shoes is expensive if you never wear them, and the cabin was downright extravagant considering that in the five years I owned it, I visited it exactly four times.

So what did I gain from that experience? Strange to say, peace of mind. Ever since I was a little girl, I had dreamed of living in a rustic cabin in the woods, a fantasy that persisted in my imagination even as I grew into a city-dwelling adult. I was shocked when I finally got what I had always wanted and found that I had no use for it. But despite the round of tsk-tsks and told-you-so's I endured from friends and family, I found the knowledge liberating.

I am completely over feeling guilty about the spoils of my feckless career as an impulse buyer.

And despite everyone's advice and exhortations, the only "lesson" I took away from my cabin experience was that if I didn't want a cabin, I'd better keep trying until I found out what I did want. I soon caused a minor scandal when I turned right around and bought myself a little sailboat. But the boat was magic. I felt like Audrey Hepburn in *Sabrina*, having fancied herself in love with the caddish William Holden all those years, only to be swept off her feet by Humphrey Bogart. Boating became a lifelong passion, and the tsk-tskers eventually clammed up and went away (they always do).

Even the chair had unexpected and serendipitous consequences, though it failed utterly and miserably to realize its original destiny as a decor item.

It may seem illogical, but I believe that even pointless impulses and useless objects have a purpose—as catalysts for change or self-discovery, if nothing else.

To understand what a bold act bringing home this chair was, you need to know that I live with a man with the aesthetic adventurousness of an 18th-century German philosopher. Immanuel Kant, for those of you who don't know the type, was so rigorously scheduled that he ate only one meal a day, at midday, and never traveled farther than 60 miles from his home; the house-wives of his town supposedly set their clocks by his passing. My aesthetic, on the other hand, is a cross between *A Clockwork Orange* and *Pirates of the Caribbean.* Which is why the only pieces of furniture to have crossed our threshold before the chair were family cast-offs that provoked no controversy simply by virtue of being free.

A Catalyst for Change

You can't imagine the horror on my boyfriend's face when I brought the chair home in the back of my Isuzu. And he didn't quite get it when I explained that, had I not bought the thing, it would have haunted me for the rest of my days, the way the One That Got Away haunts a deep-sea fisherman. Even if it turned out to be a catch-and-release purchase, I had to have it.

For the few weeks that the chair sat in our living room, we marveled at how unexpectedly comfortable and useful it was, despite its hideousness. I spent many a night curled up in it with a mystery novel, and there was just room enough for the dog to curl up beside me. Its presence made our evenings pleasant and cozy. But I knew that the chair didn't fit in and had to go (and go it did, fetching $75 on eBay). When it was finally driven away in the back of its new owner's Nissan Quest minivan, my boyfriend and I were as wistful as two accidental foster parents in a Lifetime Original Movie. Our lives had been touched.

The two of us had never really made our house a home, because we were both too stubborn to compromise our aesthetics. But the chair changed all that. Three days later, we were the proud owners of a conservative living-room set from a hotel liquidator (which made my boyfriend happy) and a shag carpet from the 70s (garish enough to suit me). All was finally well. The furniture stalemate had been broken, and now there is talk in the air of dining tables, draperies, and nightstands. None of which would be happening if I hadn't had the nerve to bring home the Ugliest Chair in the World.

It may seem illogical, but I believe that even pointless impulses and useless objects have a purpose—as catalysts for change or self-discovery, if nothing else. The question "Who am I?" is one we answer by echolocation, bouncing our identities off the things around us to see which ones speak to us and which ones don't, the noes as vital to our internal guidance system as the yesses. I have three lovely Brooks Brothers shirts in the closet to remind me who I'm not, and a kaleidoscope of paisley blouses that make me feel at home in my skin. And the next time I feel like instigating a relationship breakthrough, there's a green Lucite swag lamp at the antique mall downtown that I've had my eye on for quite some time.

10

Materialism Leads to Unhappiness

Tim Kasser

Tim Kasser is a psychology professor at Knox College and the author of The High Price of Materialism.

In consumer-oriented societies there is a correlation between materialistic values and low self-esteem. Because consumer cultures value material goods, many individuals have learned to associate purchasing the right item with well-being. This phenomenon is exacerbated when an individual has a history of unfulfilled needs. Many items within consumer culture, however, fail to meet the individual's deeper psychological needs. Like junk food, these products fail to provide real nutrition for the consumer. The attempt by the individual to meet psychological needs by purchasing material goods, then, leads to frustration, and lowers the quality of an individual's well-being.

> But Mom, I *need* that toy.
>
> —*Anonymous child*

W hen people are strongly oriented to materialistic values they also experience low well-being. But why is this true? Do materialistic values cause people's problems? If so, how? Or is it the case that people who are already unhappy focus on wealth, possessions, image, and popularity? If so, why?

The answers to these questions are clearly complicated, and the scientists' mantra, "More research is needed," has rarely been more pertinent. Yet I believe that a sound theory can be constructed to explain much of what researchers have found concerning materialism's "dark side." The theory that my colleagues and I have been developing is based in the idea of psychological needs, and it is with this concept that we must begin. . . .

Although needs provide a basic motivation to do something, they do not tell us exactly how to satisfy them. The way needs express themselves and the extent to which they are satisfied depend on a number of factors, including our personality, lifestyle, values, and the culture in which we live.

When people are strongly oriented to materialistic values they also experience low well-being.

For example, if I am hungry, my need for sustenance motivates me to eat. The way that I satisfy this need will vary depending on my personal tastes and on my environment. If I like sweet foods, I might seek out an orange or some candy; if I like salty foods, I might prefer pretzels or potato chips; if I live in Japan, I might eat sushi; if I live in Lebanon, I will be likely to eat hummus. Personality and societal context provide frameworks for need expression and satisfaction by suggesting particular pathways and behaviors we might follow. In many cases, these frameworks do a reasonably good job of satisfying our needs, and thus of supporting psychological health and well-being.

Consider what would happen, however, if every time I was hungry I ate chocolate cake; many of my body's physical needs for certain nutrients would remain unfulfilled, and my health would surely suffer. In a similar manner, it is not necessarily the case that our personalities and culture provide healthy pathways that adequately satisfy psychological needs. Instead, aspects of our personalities and life circumstances sometimes lead us to try to satisfy our needs in ways that are ultimately unfulfilling. And sometimes our environments fail to furnish many opportunities for healthy expression of our needs, and thus lead us astray from the ways of life that could really help us to be happy.

The Internalization of Consumer Culture

When we look around at contemporary consumer culture it is clear that people are constantly bombarded with messages that needs can be satisfied by having the right products. Feel unsafe on the road or in your home? Buy the right tire or lock. Worried that you will die young? Eat this cereal and take out insurance from that company just in case. Lawn look bad in comparison with your neighbor's? Buy this lawnmower and fertilizer. Can't get a date? Buy these clothes, this shampoo, and that deodorant. No adventure in your life? Take this vacation, buy that sport-utility vehicle, or subscribe to these magazines. Consumer societies also provide many role models suggesting that a high quality of life (i.e., need satisfaction) occurs when one has successfully attained material goals. Heroes and heroines of consumeristic cultures are on the whole wealthy, good-looking and often famous. These are the people, we are told, who are successful, whose lives we should strive to imitate and emulate.

When we look around at contemporary consumer culture it is clear that people are constantly bombarded with messages that needs can be satisfied by having the right products.

In the face of messages glorifying the path of consumption and wealth, all of us to some extent take on or internalize materialistic values. That is, we incorporate the messages of consumer society into our own value and belief systems. These values then begin to organize our lives by influencing the goals we pursue, the attitudes we have toward particular people and objects, and the behaviors in which we engage.

Almost all of us place at least some importance on possessions, money, and image, but materialism takes hold of the center of some people's value systems. As a consequence, their experiences will be changed. To illustrate, take two people, one who values material wealth more than helping others, and another with the opposite set of priorities. When confronted with a decision about what career to pursue, the materialistic individual will be likely to seek out a high-paying, high-status job with many opportunities to earn a great deal of money. In contrast, the less materialistic individual will be likely to accept a lower-paying job if it will benefit others. Or imagine that both individuals are presented with a special issue of *Forbes* magazine about how wealthy people obtained their riches. The materialistic person will likely read the magazine with interest, while the other individual will likely become quickly bored. What these examples show is that the two people's lives, and thus the experiences they have, are quite different as a result of their values.

The different experiences of these two individuals will influence the extent to which their needs are ultimately satisfied. Just as a person who eats junk food will be less healthy than one who eats many fruits and vegetables, an individual with relatively central materialistic values will have fewer chances to fulfill the needs required for psychological growth and happiness. . . . Materialistic values lead people into a style of life and way of experiencing that do a rather poor job of satisfying their needs. Taking our nutritional metaphor a bit farther, consumer society sells junk food, promising that it tastes good and makes us happy. As a result, many people buy it. Alas, they are full for only a short time, as the promise is false and the satisfaction is empty.

Mistaking Wealth for Happiness

Given that most of us are exposed to similar cultural messages encouraging materialism, why is it that some of us internalize these values more than others? Why did the first individual in the example above care more about wealth and possessions than the second person? One explanation involves the extent to which people have been exposed to the messages of consumer culture. For example, people are likely to be materialistic if they watch a great deal of television and if their parents value materialistic goals. So part of the answer is that some people simply learn this attitude or outlook because of their environment.

Individuals who have not had their needs well met in the past come to think that wealth and possessions will bring them happiness and a good life.

But it is also the case that people's preexisting level of need satisfaction causes them to value certain outcomes differently. As Abraham Maslow [creator of the "hierarchy of needs"] wrote, when people have a particular need that is not well satisfied, their "whole philosophy of the future tends also to change. For our chronically and extremely hungry man, Utopia can be defined simply as a place where there is plenty of food. He tends to think that, if only he is guaranteed food for the rest of his life, he will be perfectly happy and will never want anything more." The same dynamic seems to occur in the case of materialism. Individuals who have not had their needs well met in the past come to think that wealth and possessions will bring them happiness and a good life. Part of this belief is due to the fact that society tells them the material path will make them feel secure, and part is because our bodies require some material comforts to survive. In any case, a strong focus on materialistic values is often a symptom or manifestation of a personal history characterized by a relative failure in need satisfaction. These unmet needs thus lead people to be unhappy and to develop materialistic values. . . .

People have needs that must be satisfied for them to have a high quality of life. Materialistic values become prominent in the lives of some individuals who have a history of not having their needs well met. Thus, one reason these values are associated with a low quality of life is that they are symptoms or signs that some needs remain unfulfilled. But materialistic values are not just expressions of unhappiness. Instead, they lead people to organize their lives in ways that do a poor job of satisfying their needs, and thus contribute even more to people's misery.

11

Consumerism Is Empowering to Teens

Jim Pooler

Jim Pooler is a professor at the University of Saskatchewan and author of Why We Shop: Emotional Rewards and Retail Strategies.

Shopping is about making decisions, and decisions provide the consumer with a feeling of power and control. In everyday life many people within society have relatively little power; shopping, on the other hand, allows even a child to exercise power. Shoppers define themselves by displaying financial success. Shopping also empowers groups like working-class and teenage consumers. While both groups are forced to follow a manager or mom and dad's instructions on a daily basis, they are in charge when making a purchase. Shopping also fosters a sense of belonging within a given culture, with specific purchases implying membership in specific groups. Shopping, then, provides the consumer with the power to define him- or herself and to define him- or herself within the larger culture.

Shopping puts people in control. Everyday shopping is largely about making decisions, and when people shop they make a multitude of decisions, thus gaining a feeling of power and of control. Consider the housewife or househusband who is on a routine grocery-shopping expedition. The entire trip through the store requires an endless stream of decisions and represents an opportunity to be in charge, to be the one making those decisions. Shopping puts the power of decision making in the hands of the shopper. And it does not matter whether the person is otherwise largely powerless in his life—in the store the shopper is king. Shopping can put power in the hands of people who do not otherwise have it. Shopping, in other words, is empowering, whether it is for everyday groceries or for buying a new house.

People grow up with the message that shopping provides power. The young child buying penny candy in a convenience store is empowered by the fact that she has money and is able to make purchasing decisions. In fact, this may be the first real experience in life where independent decision making, on a limited budget, takes place. It gives the child control of her purchases and puts the power of her money at her disposal. The 50-year-old clerk at the store responds to the child's wishes and bends to her demands. For the first time in her life the child has power over an adult, and the message is a strong one. Money provides power, and shopping provides the outlet where one can exercise that power. . . .

The phrase we are all taught from childhood onward is that the buyer is always right. The implication is that the shopper has power. There are two forms of this power. In the first place, there is power over the shopkeeper or salesclerk. The interaction between the shopper and the salesman is such that the consumer is the one who is supposed to be in control. It is the shopper who should place demands on the salesclerk and who should dictate the course of the sales transaction. Of course, this is not always the case when it comes to pushy salesclerks and high-pressure salesmen. But by and large, the salesclerk is taught to demur to the customer's whims, wishes, and desires. If the customer wants to try on more clothes, drive another test car, or see another television, the salesman is usually happy to oblige in order to keep the customer happy and, eventually, make the sale. The power is in the hands of the customer, who holds the sword of the potential purchase over the salesman's head. This is especially true in those situations where the salesperson gets a commission when he or she makes a sale. This is also true whether the shopper is 7 years old or 70 years old.

Wealth Equals Power

But there is also another form of power in shopping. Being able to own the biggest, or best, or newest of anything has traditionally been associated with power. The logic of this relationship is easy. Wealth is power. That power is exercised through possessions. Wealthy people demonstrate their power and place in society by the results of their shopping. The wealthy usually have the biggest houses, the best furnishings, the most expensive vehicles, and so on. Shopping is the means whereby people are able to express their station in life through what they buy. Whether one drives a brand-new Lincoln Navigator, or a 15-year-old Toyota Tercel, one is displaying one's financial accomplishments in life. A person's possessions are taken as one important measure of that individual's success in life, and whether we like it or not, wealth is ultimately equated with power. Thus the shopper also has power over the salesclerk by virtue of his assets.

Shopping can put power in the hands of people who do not otherwise have it.

Although the wealth of the shopper is not always evident to sales personnel, very often the means of the shopper can be estimated by the very nature of the products she looks at or the stores she frequents. The low-end shopper frequents the discount stores and bargain outlets looking for low-priced, everyday merchandise. Meanwhile, the high-end shopper patronizes shops that are upscale, in search of goods that are sophisticated and out of the ordinary. The everyday shopper fights the crowds. The sales staff is overworked, underpaid, and sometimes indifferent. At the same time, the wealthy shopper frequents expensive boutiques where the sales staffs are attentive, knowledgeable, and eager to please. The wealthy consumer is likely to buy more and spend more, and thus has the undivided attention of store staff.

Part of the logic of the power relationship in shopping comes from the idea of the commissioned salesman. Everyone has had the experience of the too-pushy salesman, and most people assume this means that the salesman is on commission. But what does the commission accomplish? In essence it *gives the shopper more power*. The salesman working on commission is at the beck and call of the customer: such a salesman is more anxious than others are to make the sale, and as a consequence this puts more power than normal in the hands of the shopper. Often the shopper sees a salesman on commission as being pushy, when in fact the customer should view such occasions as a chance to exert greater than usual control over sales personnel. Of course, this is easier said than done, but the fact remains that the commissioned salesperson is more desperate to make a sale and should be seen as such.

Consumerism Empowers the Powerless

Perhaps the best example of the way in which shopping is empowering is seen in the low- to middle-income shopper. This is the average couple who both have regular jobs where they carry out the same repetitive tasks from day to day. It may be a boring job but it earns a decent income, puts food on the table and earns its owner a healthy measure of self-respect and pride. Most such working people take orders from someone else all day long, every day, and are seldom put in any position of decision-making authority. For such people, life consists of a job where the boss is king. But there is a major exception to this rule. The one big exception is shopping. In the evenings and on weekends when it comes time to shop, the regular working man or woman is suddenly given the power to make decisions. Some of these are small, and others are large, but shopping gives the average working person a chance to be in control and make important decisions. This is the primary empowering capability of shopping and its significance should not be overlooked. Shopping levels the playing field and gives everyone the power to become important.

Shopping levels the playing field and gives everyone the power to become important.

A case in point is found in the teenager who is shopping for clothes, shoes, and accessories. When these teens are younger their clothing is purchased for them, and chosen for them, by their parents. But there comes a time when preteens start to want to buy their own clothes and, more importantly, want to start to make *their own decisions*. Part of the blossoming life of the young preteen comes from *attaining the power* to do one's own shopping. This is usually a difficult time in life for adults and children alike. Parents who have always traditionally been in control of what their children wear suddenly find themselves faced not only with a rebellious preteen but also with a loss of decision-making power. Children wrench this power from their parents whether the parents like it or not. It is part of growing up. Similarly, children who have always been dressed by their parents start to resent the lack of control they have over how they look and start to resist the power of their parents in deciding what they will wear. Battles ensue. Although these often appear to be about clothing and appearance, they are actually about power. Who has the power to decide what will be worn, the parent or the child? Right or wrong, the preteen wants the *power* to make his or her own shopping decisions. He or she wants this measure of independence from parental control. *The clothes themselves are secondary*—the main point is for the preteen to begin to earn his or her independence as an adult by making his or her own clothing-shopping decisions.

There are not many areas of life in which a preteen or teen can assert independence or make decisions. They are surrounded by authority figures, such as parents and teachers, virtually every minute of the day. Their life is highly structured and seldom do they get to express themselves as individual and unique human beings. Yet they are at a stage in life when this is very important to them. They are searching for the means to be able to declare themselves as unique and important people who are not just clones of their parents' desires. They want to become individuals. Shopping lets them accomplish this.

Little children wear exactly what their parents want them to, and so are just reflections of how their parents see them as people. Their choice of dress has little to do with how they see themselves. Preteens break free of the shackles of their clothing servitude by rebelling against the control that their parents exert and by making their own shopping and dress decisions. In the highly constrained life of the teen and preteen, clothing is one area where individual expression is maximized. This is one of the few areas where the teen is able to declare, "This is me. This is who I am as a unique individual." This is very important in life, and adults, teens, and retailers alike should be aware that it is an essential component of growing up. This is not just shopping—this is a crucial part of the transition from childhood to adulthood. It is one of the most important reasons for shopping.

In order for parents to understand the teen's point of view, one need only remind adults of the freedom and power they have with their own shopping.

Advertisers would be well advised to take this perspective into account when they target preteen and teen audiences.

The message should be that buying a certain product is not just about fashion; rather, it is an assertion of personal independence. In a life that is otherwise highly structured, clothing, shoes, and accessories should be marketed as items that provide the means to assert oneself as a person, rather than as a clone of one's parents.

In order for parents to understand the teen's point of view, one need only remind adults of the freedom and power they have with their own shopping. If adults get the urge to purchase a particular piece of clothing for any reason whatsoever, they are usually free to do so. They are free to open their wallets and make a very personal decision about what to buy and what to wear. Imagine if those same adults could only buy or wear what someone else approved of—and that someone else had very different ideas about what they should wear. Teens and preteens are looking to have the same freedom to choose that adults have. Wise parents should remember that when it comes time to do battle over clothing, teens are simply looking for the same freedom that they themselves already have. . . .

Shopping as Belonging

Sociologists tell us that one of the important human needs is to feel a sense of belonging to one or more groups in life. Thus the average person may feel that they belong to a number of groups such as with coemployees, with social groups or friends, with community groups or sports teams, with neighbors, and so on. In essence, we all belong to a number of different social groups and the sense of belonging and camaraderie that is created is important to our mental well-being. Shopping is a key to many group memberships, whether they are formal or informal, and a big part of the feeling of belongingness that people need is often achieved through buying things.

Very often membership in a group implies that it is necessary to *purchase* items to establish affiliation with that group.

There are many subtle and not-so-subtle ways in which people establish group membership, but almost all of them involve the purchase of something. Consider membership in a sports team, athletic club, exercise group, and so on. Items such as clothing, equipment, or membership fees usually need to be purchased in order to belong to the group. For instance, a man who is a member of a sports team will need to acquire equipment, a uniform, and perhaps a team jacket to become part of the group. He will also probably need to pay user fees or membership dues to be able to participate in an activity. Thus, group membership comes at a price and usually part of that membership requires the purchase of several things. Similarly, a woman who is a member of an aerobics class will need to purchase appropriate work-out clothing and will need to pay a membership fee in order to become part of the group.

Very often membership in a group implies that it is necessary to purchase items to establish affiliation with that group.

Sometimes membership in a group is defined by the very things that the participants own. Car clubs, gun clubs, model clubs, craft clubs, and so on are associations where ownership of the appropriate equipment or materials is essential to participation in the group. Group identity comes from belonging to a collective with shared interests, but more important than the interests themselves is the sense of belongingness and camaraderie that is created. Thus, owning certain things, and buying certain things, ultimately leads to the achievement of a feeling of membership in a social group. Shopping for these items is a means to an end.

Clothing and Group Identity

There are many more subtle and interesting ways in which people purchase group membership. One of the more important ones comes through the way in which people dress. For instance, in the working environment of an office, there is usually an unwritten dress code for employees. People usually follow such an informal dress code rigorously, and by so doing they define group membership for themselves. Employees at different levels of seniority may define their different group membership by their dress code. For example, men in middle-level management may find it adequate to wear a tie and sports coat, while upper-level managers may find it appropriate to wear suits. This type of dress code behavior creates an environment where group membership is quite clearly defined by the clothing people wear. Lines of authority and communication reflect the boundaries set out by the different clothing styles.

Clothing defines group membership much more broadly than just within the confines of the workplace. All people define themselves and their group memberships by the way they dress. In extreme cases, one can imagine members of motorcycle gangs or religious sects where group membership is clearly defined by the style of clothing that members wear. The same is true, more or less, of everyone. People define their place in life, and their group affiliations, by the way they dress. Shopping for and purchasing particular clothing entitles one to informal membership in a group. This is true whether one considers a group of men playing golf or fishing, a group of women playing golf or hosting a baby shower, or a group of teens going to a movie together. In all of these cases, there is a commonality of dress code that makes the wearers feel that they belong to the group they are with. This feeling of belongingness is very important in life and is brought about in large part by the clothing, shoes, and accessories that people purchase everyday.

There are many levels for which shopping time is invested in creating a sense of belongingness. Most people belong to a large number of different groups, both formal and informal.

The middle manager who dresses her role at work may belong to a fitness club and a sports team in the evenings, and she may also belong to a community association and a church choir on the weekend. Every one of these activities requires a different and unique dress code, and shopping effort will be expended to satisfy the demands of each group.

12

Materialism Undermines the Family

Patricia Dalton

Patricia Dalton is a clinical psychologist in private practice in Washington, D.C.

Once, only a minority of people were wealthy. In America today, however, even the average middle-class consumer has an abundance of possessions. Far from making Americans happier, though, the need to acquire material goods has placed more stress on families. Today, parents work longer hours, leaving less time for home life. As a result, both marriages and parent-children relationships suffer. Children have reacted by either becoming more status conscious or by rejecting status altogether. By confusing wants with needs, American families have forgotten that material gain, ultimately, cannot make one happy.

On the biggest shopping weekend of the year, many of us are beset by a dilemma: what to buy for the person who has everything. It makes me think of the teenager I heard about in my psychotherapy office, who opened a gift from his 90-year-old great-aunt, tossed it aside and said, "I already have that."

Many of us already "have that." We have become, to borrow a phrase President Bush used while addressing his donors, "the haves and the have mores." That explains why some of us are left feeling spiritually empty during this season of feasting and giving.

There have always been the few who live lavishly, with estates, servants and multiple homes, just as there have always been some who struggle to get by with very little. But having a lot is no longer the province of the few. Acquisition—and its close companion, acquisition envy—is a problem not just for the elite but also for the average person. I see the impact day after day among the people who come to my office for counseling. Relationships among family members and between friends are suffering. We've become materially richer but interpersonally poorer.

My colleagues and I talk about the repetitive patterns of acquisitive behavior we observe on a daily basis. We see high school girls carrying Prada bags that are not knockoffs and competing with one another through their apparel. We hear from adolescents who get caught shoplifting and others who get away with it (and these are kids who have disposable money and don't need new clothes). We listen to adults describing patterns of what I call "comfort shopping"—buying clothes they don't need and never wear and that sit in their closets with the tags on. We hear from single people whose spending habits put them so deeply into credit card debt that they end up declaring bankruptcy. Members of one family told me that they can identify at least three successive generations of compulsive shoppers and still find it hard to resist the siren song of the mall.

Materialism's Toll on Family Life

There's a change I've witnessed in the 20-plus years I've been in practice. People used to buy things when they needed them; now they buy things when they want them or want their children to have them. Adolescents in the past were rarely presented with new cars on their 16th birthdays, but it's not uncommon today. Kids used to buy cars when they could afford them—usually of the beat-up, secondhand variety. Now, at a time in their lives when they are both vulnerable and easily influenced, teenagers find themselves behind the wheels of powerful, expensive machines, ill-prepared to handle the repercussions of a fender bender, much less a serious accident.

If there were evidence that increasing affluence made people happier, there might be occasion to rejoice. Even though GDP [gross domestic product] per capita has tripled since World War II, and houses have grown bigger, cars more luxurious, clothing and food easier to afford, we seem to be working mindlessly to acquire more. In fact, there is ample evidence, both anecdotal and scientific, that once people attain a reasonably good standard of living, making more money and buying more has no appreciable positive effect and in some cases has negative effects.

Acquisition—and its close companion, acquisition envy—is a problem not just for the elite but also for the average person.

The biggest cost I see is intergenerational. Materialism is taking a drastic toll at home. There is considerable strain involved in generating the money needed to acquire so much. Many of the parents who come to my office describe living on the earn-and-spend, earn-and-spend treadmill that Berkeley sociologist Arlie Hochschild describes. Parents are exhausted. Children are neglected. Marriages get put on hold. One professional woman reported to me that she felt so overwhelmed that she came home one evening and started breaking plates on the floor in front of her three little kids. Stories like this make me realize we are allowing ourselves to be robbed of what is most precious and counts the most: free time.

Some families manage to survive the grueling parental work schedules needed to maintain or increase the standard of living. Others succumb. Sometimes the marriage is the casualty; sometimes it's a child; sometimes both. I can remember a former competitive swimmer who applied her all-training-all-the-time approach to her business. She seemed to be addicted to relentless activity and the accoutrements it would then allow her to buy. Her husband told her he'd leave her if she didn't spend more time at home. She didn't—and he did. The big house they had been able to buy simply didn't make up for her absence.

Parents with No Time

One sad story I've seen in countless variations goes like this: A father puts in punishing hours at the job, believing he is doing the best for his family. The children, who rarely saw their busy father when they were young, see him even less as they grow up surrounded by toys, and the marriage falters and dissolves. The dad feels misunderstood when the children come up with excuses not to see him. One father told me indignantly that he now felt like a money machine; in reality, it was just the old pattern continuing.

Some families manage to survive the grueling parental work schedules needed to maintain or increase the standard of living. Others succumb.

The desire for the material and social status that comes with successful careers leads to one of the worst situations therapists encounter—that of a child with two parents, neither of whom has time for him or her. I can remember a boy who spent far more time with the nanny and gardener (who didn't speak English) than with his high-powered mother and father. They spoke glowingly of their jobs and extensive travel and social life and second home, but neither was willing to change their acquisitive lifestyle for a simpler life with their child, who was exhibiting serious symptoms as a little boy. A young adult patient I saw with a similar history described this kind of parent as MIA, or missing in action.

More young people are questioning their parents' way of life. I can think of one patient raised in Chevy Chase whose father wanted him to follow in his footsteps, assuming that he would continue the family's upward mobility. The son told me that, after some thought, he realized it wasn't for him. He felt that the lifestyle hadn't even been particularly satisfying for his father. Instead, he has become a self-employed carpenter and lives on a houseboat. (In an act of reverse materialism, he recently sold the family antiques to a dealer, because he'll never need them.)

It defies common sense to assume that each generation will be able to have more than the last. At some point, the trajectory will inevitably change. One of my girlfriends leaned over to me when we were having dinner recently and said, "I'm afraid that my kids think I'm cheap." I called her the next day and told her that, actually, I think they're lucky. They have a mom who has helped prepare them for a future in which their fortunes (and that of their nation) may rise or fall. Thriftiness has survival value.

The biggest price being paid for rampant materialism may be within families, but I am also struck by the competitive edge this preoccupation lends to relationships between contemporaries. Items take on enormous symbolic importance. Of course it happens to people of all ages (everyone knows a man who covets another's sports car or a woman who wants her neighbor's granite countertops), but children and teenagers are the most vulnerable.

I am seeing a new level of competitiveness, not just on the athletic fields and in the classroom but increasingly over possessions. I think of it as the Keds-to-Nike transformation. One status-conscious teenage girl (whose parents checked out my diplomas before they even sat down) said she couldn't understand why she had trouble making and keeping friends. This girl had learned much more about domination than cooperation, and she formed alliances to get what she wanted rather than making real friends.

Wealth Does Not Equal Happiness

The scientific literature supports my office observations. A comprehensive review of more than 150 studies on happiness and wealth by psychologists Ed Diener and Martin Seligman showed that there has been no appreciable rise in life satisfaction over the past decades, despite our increased material wealth.

The Alfred P. Sloan Foundation issued a report that is sure to give ambitious and acquisitive parents pause. It found an inverse relationship between self-reported child happiness and parental income. Blue-collar and middle-class kids identified themselves as happier than wealthy ones. Kids need their parents on site—in the foreground when they are young, and in the background as they get older. That's simply not possible in many of today's go-getter households.

In our increasingly materialistic culture, needs and wants have become one and the same.

So here we are: a generation of fashionistas and Samurai shoppers with full closets and empty hearts. Instead of listening to our souls, we have fallen for a new field of retail anthropology that advises businesses on how to get people in the mood to buy, buy, buy. I saw a catchy phrase that headlined an article in this newspaper's business section several months ago: Appliance Lust. It referred to hunger for eight-burner Viking ranges, built-in woks and Sub-Zero refrigerators with custom wood paneling and door alarms. Those of us who lived through the '60s seem to have forgotten the warning that everything you buy owns you.

In our increasingly materialistic culture, needs and wants have become one and the same. When I see people in my office who are struggling to figure out what is most important to them, I often ask them to imagine being on their deathbed, looking back over their lives. What will they rejoice in? What will fall in the neutral category? And what will they regret? Does all this stuff make people more contented with their lives? Apparently not. And after all, as the saying goes, you can't take it with you.

13

Materialism Has Led to a Credit Culture

Brett Williams

Brett Williams is a professor of anthropology at American University. She is the author of Upscaling Downtown: Stalled Gentrification in Washington, D.C.

While many people rely on the convenience of credit cards, many others use them to maintain a modest lifestyle. Easy credit, however, has served to mask falling incomes and economic inequality in the United States since the 1970s. When debtors find themselves in financial difficulty, the culture at large blames the debtor and not the institutions that have extended credit. In truth, a handful of wealthy institutions, charging excessive rates, have created the current credit crisis. Debtors, like other consumers, need to organize to protect their rights.

Some people use credit cards to order concert tickets by telephone, pay for reimbursed travel in advance, keep a record of their income tax deductions, settle large bills a month after purchase so that the money can sit in an interest-bearing account, get free insurance and theft protection, and fly free. Other people pay high interest to maintain a modest standard of living; repair their cars; pay medical bills, utility bills, and tuition; buy durables and groceries; survive widowhood, divorce, and other life transitions; or gamble on enrichment programs like piano and soccer lessons that might give their children a boost to a more secure and abundant life. Many Americans settle for the facades, the illusions, of middle class lives as expensive credit drags us down, and unproductive investment in debt saps the energy of the economy.

Credit and debt lure and distract us from the real reasons households face economic crisis.

We may hate our debt and feel complicit for carrying it, we may be driven crazy trying to elude our creditors, but we have not mobilized our anger at the people and institutions that have choked us with debt. Instead, many of us blame the poor, the welfare state, greedy and impulsive women, or racially marked and foreign others. Despite the many legal instruments that allow the rich to preserve and pass on great fortunes; despite the nearly perfect, cradle-to-grave socialist cocoon of support and protection provided military officers and veterans; and despite handsome mortgage and educational subsidies for the middle class many Americans appear to believe that it is poor people, usually black women, who defy cultural values emphasizing the importance of self-sufficiency and leech off the state. Credit and debt lure and distract us from the real reasons households face economic crisis. We feel grateful that credit cards allow us to go to college or that the pawnbroker financed a prescription or that a payday loan made Christmas possible. People who do not pay interest often confront their "credit others" across a moral divide: other people who pay interest confirm their claims to moral superiority.

Credit is part of the ebb and flow of social life, for nobody is or can be or should be truly self-sufficient. Credit allows people to extend the here and now, to ease transitions, plant crops, go fishing, sell goods in markets, move to a new place, or invest in capital equipment by taking on an obligation to repay the loan during flusher times. Credit can take such simple forms as carpooling or be as complex as the Trobrianders' kula ring, which bound people on dispersed islands in a social web of delayed ceremonial exchanges of arm bands for necklaces.

Credit and Debt Are About Power

Credit and debt are also grimly implicated in power relations. People take on debt to large lending institutions in the corporate world. When inequalities between debtors and creditors are too stark, people may enter a modern form of peonage, as they pay for debt by being in hock with their lives, or experience usury when the interest on the debt is so great that it unjustly saps the debtor and perpetuates the inequalities that made it necessary in the first place. Colonial encounters, when indigenous peoples labored to pay for goods they never wanted; sharecropping, when laborers worked to pay for the soil and the seed money that allowed them to plant; human smuggling, which deposits immigrants and sex workers in a new place where they must labor, undocumented, to pay for transport, or structural adjustment programs requiring that developing nations slash social services and domestic industries to secure international loans—all illustrate the unjust power relations and lasting suffering inflicted and buttressed by peonage and usury.

The illusion of choice and our own feelings of complicity hide the fact that debt is embodied domination, that the purpose of consumer credit is to keep you in debt in perpetuity.

Credit and debt only make sense in the context of other social relations and obligations, and anthropologists have long been interested in the broader context of which debt is a part. Credit is not a gift, but from the creditor's perspective it can act like one. Gifts can be insurance policies or savings accounts, a way to hedge your bets for your own hard times, because gifts often carry with them a statement about a relationship as well as the obligation to give something back.

Credit also implies a relationship of a sort. It can express solidarity and interdependence because you are a member of a gang, a clan, or you are an in-law or *compadre*. Debts may bind you and your group to another group over time as, for example, when Nuer families pay bride wealth cattle to their in-laws for many years to compensate them for the loss of childbearing women. Debt throws you off balance in some way, for there is always a time lag and an asymmetry involved. The crucial questions become Were you dragged into debt or did you ask for credit willingly? When do you have to pay it back, to whom are you indebted, and what sanctions are available to the creditor? Does it lift you up or drag you down, *and is that the essential difference between credit and debt* ? Are they the same thing, with the difference in how you experience and perceive it? Are they always double edged, expressing solidarity and separateness, reciprocity and power, promise and threat? Do they go on forever, or do they end, and how do they end if they ever do?

Credit Obscures Income Inequality

In the United States during the last thirty years, these relations have been so masked that they are almost unrecognizable. We have no cultural language to understand and interpret them, so we often liken credit to freedom and mastery, and debt to addiction, drug abuse, narcissism, low self-esteem, dependency, or a search for immediate gratification. We tend to blame the debtors rather than the institutions that did the irresponsible lending. "Debt porn" fills the pages of popular magazines, where readers can learn about the folly that trapped other people in a downward spiral of debt and memorize the steps that will help them get out. Without debtors' prisons, the end is less sure: we hope for a miraculous change in fortune, the death of a relative, an unusually good year in commissions. Perhaps we'll hit the lottery, find the right consolidation/repayment plan, or file for bankruptcy protection.

There are better metaphors for the relationship between expensive credit and debt: welfare in a lost welfare state or domestic partners in a declining economy where deflated households need more than one worker. The apparently anachronistic concepts of usury and peonage still work too. We live in the most unequal society in the industrialized West. The richest 20 percent of Americans earn nine times more than the poorest 20 percent, and the richest 1 percent of the richest group hold 38 percent of its wealth. Wealthy, powerful institutions extend expensive credit for excessive profits. Credit cards act to obscure, reproduce, and exacerbate divisions of class. race, and gender by creating a credit relationship in which individuals and banks are paired in a patronizing, asymmetrical economy of debt. The illusion of choice and our own feelings of complicity hide the fact that debt is embodied domination, that the purpose of consumer credit is to keep you in debt in perpetuity. You are not supposed to be able to pay enough to escape debt, but you are supposed to pay interest on time or be disciplined by higher interest, penalties, fees, and harping, dunning, threats, and infantilizing phone calls. Your detailed, precise credit history can be stigmatizing or enabling: it is your life, it legitimizes you. Your credit report is accepted as an objective measure of citizenship and personal financial responsibility; it is a seamless, convenient means of reproducing inequality.

We debtors need to organize too. We need to insist that being a citizen does not mean being a consumer.

In 1976 when my first unsolicited credit card arrived in the mail, I immediately treated my neighbor and her three sons to dinner at the Cuban restaurant on our block. None of us had any money—she worked as a maid and I was a new assistant professor—and the experience felt magical to us. During the years since, I have marveled that the changes I describe here came so quickly to seem like the natural state of affairs. Despite faithfully reading everything from the *Journal of Retail Banking* to the *Left Business Observer*, despite interviewing dozens of despairing debtors, every financial decision I have made during these years has been a bad one. Trying to cushion the shock of my husband's death, I used credit cards to make sure my children would not be materially deprived on top of their grief. I took on a mortgage I couldn't pay. I bought a nice car and twice pawned it. I took on ill-paying projects to make extra money. Those few friends and relatives I wasn't too ashamed to tell about my struggles bailed me out again and again. I have had judgments brought against me and my salary garnished. I still carry debt, and I will probably always be in debt, although I have not used credit cards in a very long time. I rent a house in a poor neighborhood, and I cannot afford a car. When my sons went to college, despite their mother's experiences, they quickly acquired their own credit cards and maxed them out. I reveal these personal experiences to make very clear the distinction between doing social and economic analysis and living our daily lives. I do not think I am smarter than those of you who may read it. My research has not enabled me to connect the public to the private in a way that might protect my own family from the ravages—the despair, depression, guilt, shame, insomnia, and nightmares—that plague a life in debt. In many ways, I have been an unwilling participant-observer in the social relations I describe. At the same time, my class has protected me. I am a privileged debtor. . . .

Debtors Need to Organize

Although I try to duck the debt collector when she calls my house every day, I also know that MBNA is the prime mover behind the bankruptcy bill that Congress will likely pass. I can almost laugh at my disappointment in Senate cosponsor Tom Daschle, who represents the state that repealed its usury law to lure credit card operations there. Bankruptcy, if not quite a reform of the system, did give debtors a shot at a fresh start. Under the new law, everyone will have to pay more in fees, many will lose their houses and cars, many will not be able to file at all, and many who do file will come out owing exactly the same amount that they filed to escape in the first place. This bill will not affect Chapter 11 filers like Enron and World-Com, only those people paying usurious interest for groceries, medical care, car repairs, or to survive being laid off from corporations like Enron and WorldCom. It will be sent for approval to President Bush, whose top campaign contributor was MBNA.

We debtors need to organize too. We need to insist that being a citizen does not mean being a consumer. We all participate in the same economy. We are all connected to one another. The big borrowers who spent their money on financial services, junk bonds, mergers, takeovers, and leveraged buyouts in a flurry of flexible accumulation also abandoned the productive investment that would have kept our cities livable, our water clean, housing decent, trains running, children vaccinated, education meaningful, and jobs life sustaining. This book is about the connections between credit and debt, power and inequality, the Ponzi schemes in the boardroom and the power tool in the pawnshop.

14

Materialism Leads to a Lack of Community

John De Graaf, David Wann, and Thomas H. Naylor

John De Graaf is the coordinator of Take Back Your Time Day, an organization encouraging Americans to spend less time on the job. David Wann is an ecologist and author of Deep Design. *Thomas H. Naylor is a professor at Duke University and coauthor of* Downsizing the U.S.A.

The excessive consumption of the middle class in the United States has undermined both family relationships and community ties. As Americans worked harder to pay for the American Dream, they lost vital connections that had once held communities together. Volunteerism declined, and local businesses, operated by community members, were pushed aside for large chains such as Wal-Mart and Home Depot. As neighborhoods disintegrated, Americans also worried about urban crime, leading many to further isolate themselves by moving to gated neighborhoods. Far from making Americans happy, the cost of obtaining the American Dream has led to disconnection.

> *Everyplace looks like no place, and no place looks like home.*
>
> —*James Kuntsler, author of* The Geography of Nowhere

You may have seen the ad. It's . . . for an SUV. It pictures a suburban street of identical, expensive ranch style houses with perfect lawns. The SUV being advertised is parked in the driveway of one of them. But in every other driveway is . . . a tank. A real tank. A big, deadly Army tank. It's a chilling ad, meant to remind us of how chilly our communities have become as our war of all-against-all consumer competition intensifies. Psychologically, it suggests that we need to drive something as strong as a tank to compete with all the other killer vehicles out there. But a classy, comfortable tank. Of course, the ad is an exaggeration. Our communities aren't this cold and hostile. Not yet. But there's a definite chill in the air. . . .

During the 1950s, Dave [David Wann] used to walk with his grandfather four or five blocks to the town square in Crown Point, Indiana, where the older man lived. Everyone knew his grandfather, even the guy carrying a sack of salvaged goods. Forty-five years later, Dave still remembers the names of his grandparents' neighbors, and the summer backyard parties they threw. But a sense of place and the trust that comes with it are disappearing from our towns and neighborhoods.

In 1951, we sat together with the neighbors, laughing at Red Skelton. In 1985, we still watched *Family Ties* as a family. But by 1995, each member of the family often watched his or her own TV as isolation and passivity became a way of life. What began as a quest for the good life in the suburbs degenerated into private consumption splurges that separated one neighbor from another, and one family member from another. We began to feel lost in our own neighborhoods. Huge retailers took advantage of the confusion, expanding to meet our demands for cheap underwear, hardware, and software.

The more we chased bargains and the paychecks that bought them, the more vitality slipped away from our towns. Now, if we want to experience Main Street—the way it was in the good old days—we travel to Disneyworld, to a faux community where smiling shopkeepers, the slow pace, and the quaintness remind us that our real communities were once close-knit and friendly.

How will Disney portray the good old days of the suburbs in future exhibits? Will they orchestrate background ambience—highway traffic, leaf blowers, and beeping garbage trucks—to make it more realistic? Will they recreate gridlock as "bumper-to-bumper cars," complete with cell phones to tell our families we'll be late for the next ride? Will our tour of the "gated community" require more tickets than rides through the "inner city" do? Will recreational and business opportunities that have sprung up in recent years be dramatized—businesses like Kid Shuttle, a taxi service for kids whose moms aren't home to take them to Tae Kwon Do? Will Disney hire extras to play the roles of other suburbanites who can't drive—elderly, disabled, and low-income residents, peeking out from behind living-room curtains?

From Citizens to Consumers

Where can America's stranded nondrivers go in today's world? There's no colorful café down the block, or bowling alley or tavern, where neighbors can "be apart together, and mutually withdraw from the world," in the words of writer Ray Oldenburg. Such "great good places" or "third places," that are apart from both home and work environments, are now often illegal—violations of zoning codes. The truth is, the term "community life" is perceived as archaic in a world so dominated by business and government.

What began as a quest for the good life in the suburbs degenerated into private consumption splurges that separated one neighbor from another, and one family member from another.

"We've mutated from citizens to consumers in the last sixty years," says James Kuntsler, author of *The Geography of Nowhere.* "The trouble with being consumers is that consumers have no duties or responsibilities or obligations to their fellow consumers. Citizens do. They have the obligation to care about their fellow citizens, and about the integrity of the town's environment and history."

Harvard political scientist Robert Putnam has devoted his career to the study of "social capital," the connections among people that bind a community together. He observed that the quality of governance varies with the level of involvement in such things as voter turnout, newspaper readership, and membership in choral societies. Recently, he captured the public's imagination by concluding that far too many Americans are "bowling alone" (compared to a generation ago, more people are bowling, but fewer of them bowl in leagues). Once a nation of joiners, we've now become a nation of loners. Only about half of the nation's voters typically vote in presidential elections. Only thirteen percent reported attending public meetings on town or school affairs, and PTA participation has fallen from more than twelve million in 1964 to seven million in 1995. The League of Women Voters' membership is down forty-two percent since 1969, and fraternal organizations like the Elks and Lions are endangered species. Volunteering for Boy Scouts is off twenty-six percent since 1970, and for the Red Cross, sixty-one percent. Overall, a record 109 million Americans are volunteering, but many of them do it "on the run," in shorter installments, so the total time volunteered has actually declined. The "fun factor" is a major stimulant in volunteering. If it's not fun, forget it. A 1998 study on volunteering revealed that thirty percent of young adults volunteered because it was fun, compared to eleven percent who said they were committed to the cause.

Putnam concedes that membership has expanded in newer organizations such as the Sierra Club and the American Association of Retired Persons. But most members never even meet, he points out—they just pay their dues and maybe read the organization's newsletter. Internet chat groups, however convenient, are also faceless and fleshless. "Face-to-face connections are clearly more effective for building trust," he says. "Knowing the person you're talking to and taking personal responsibility for your view are crucial to having a conversation about public affairs."

The Chaining of America

Another symptom of civic degeneration is the disappearance of traditional civic leaders of community organizations. Bank presidents and business owners with long-standing ties to the community are bounced from positions of community leadership when the U.S. Banks, Wal-Marts, Office Maxes, and Home Depots come to town to put them out of business. And what do we get when the chains take over? Lower prices, cheaper stuff. But what we lose is the value of community—a nonmaterial value, but more important for a high quality of life. We lose the personal touch.

For example, small businesses give a higher percentage of their revenues to charitable organizations than the big, absentee franchises do, and they offer a lot more in terms of local character and product diversity. At a locally owned coffee shop, you might see artwork from someone who lives down the street. The shop is *your* coffee shop. At your independent bookseller, you stand a much greater chance of finding books from small presses who publish a wider variety of books than mainstream publishers.

The "chaining of America" has happened so quickly that it's hard to believe the statistics. In 1972, independent booksellers claimed fifty-eight percent of all book sales, but by 1997, their share had fallen to just seventeen percent, and it continues to fall. Lowe's and Home Depot control more than a quarter of the hardware market, forcing many a neighborhood "Mr. Fixit" to wear corporate apron colors—if he's not "over-qualified." There are similar statistics for pharmacies, 11,000 of which have recently disappeared, as well as video stores, coffee shops, and office supply stores.

Overall, more than half a million franchise businesses in sixty different industries control thirty-five percent of the retail market. By using economies of scale in purchasing and distribution, and being able to stay in the market even at a loss, the corporate retailers can drive out competition within a year, and in some cases less.

Another symptom of civic degeneration is the disappearance of traditional civic leaders of community organizations.

In search of better buys and higher tax revenues, consumers and city council members typically sacrifice first Strip Avenue, then downtown to the franchise developers, forgetting that much of a franchise dollar is electronically transferred to corporate headquarters, while a dollar spent at the local hardware stays put in towns or neighborhoods. The value of the local dollar is multiplied many times as small businesses hire architects, designers, woodworkers, sign makers, local accountants, insurance brokers, computer consultants, attorneys, advertising agencies—all services that the big retailers contract out nationally. Local retailers and distributors also carry a higher percentage of locally made goods than the chains, creating more jobs for local producers. When we buy from the chains, instead of a multiplier effect, we get a "divider effect."

In the year 2001 our social defenses are down. Distracted by material things and out of touch with social health, we watch community life from the sidelines. Hurrying to work, we see a fleet of bulldozers leveling a familiar open area next to the river, but we haven't heard yet what's going in there. Chances are good it's Wal-Mart, McDonald's, and Starbucks. . . .

Fortress America

What happens when affluenza causes communities to be pulled apart (for example, when a company leaves town and lays off hundreds of people), or crippled by bad design? We "cocoon," retreating further and further inward, and closing the gate behind us. Including secured apartment dwellers, residents of gated communities, prison inmates, and residential security system zealots, at least a fifth of the country now lives behind bars. "Socially, the house fortress represents a self-fulfilling prophecy," says community designer Peter Calthorpe. "The more isolated people become and the less they share with others unlike themselves, the more they do have to fear."

Distracted by material things and out of touch with social health, we watch community life from the sidelines.

Sociologist Edward Blakely would agree. "We are a society whose purported goal is to bring people of all income levels and races together, but gated communities are the direct opposite of that," he writes in the book *Fortress America.* "How can the nation have a social contract without having social contact?" If gated enclaves are the final act of secession from the wider community and a retreat from the civic system, 20,000 such communities, housing almost nine million people, have already seceded. Why have so many retreated from the wider community? Don't we trust each other? In 1958, trust was sky-high. Seventy-three percent of Americans surveyed said they trusted the federal government to do what is right either "most of the time" or "just about always." By 1996–1997, that percentage had fallen to less than thirty percent. It's the same with trust among individuals. Sixty percent now believe "you can't be too careful in dealing with people." It's the same story in the workplace, where the lack of trust is costly. "When we can't trust our employees or other market players," writes Robert Putnam, "we end up squandering our wealth on surveillance equipment, compliance structures, insurance, legal services, and enforcement of government regulations."

A 2000 nationwide poll conducted by the Pew School of Journalism reflected a collective queasiness in America. Compared to the ninety-six percent who felt safe in their homes, twenty percent did *not* feel safe in their own neighborhoods and thirty percent did *not* feel safe at the mall. What do these results say about the world "out there?" Grab the take-out dinner, survive the commute, just get home. In the poll, a wide sampling of Americans was asked, "What do you think is the most important problem facing the community where you live?" Predictably, crime/violence scored the highest, but surprisingly, it shared top ranking with development/sprawl/traffic/roads. Both are problems that many Americans feel are "out of control." And in an effort to regain control, we revert to the primal responses of fight or flight.

We try to fight crime with judicial and enforcement industries that have become seven percent of the U.S. economy. In recent years we've expanded the number of men and women in police uniforms to control crime and hired three times as many "rent-a-cops" as real cops. And in prisons, taxpayers pick up the tab for costs per prisoner that are comparable to sending a student to Harvard.

In any densely populated area, you'll hear the sounds of insecurity. Car alarms, beeping electronic locks, and police sirens reveal our futile quest to control crime. In reality, despite popular perceptions, living in suburbia may be statistically riskier than living in the inner city, because suburban residents drive three times as much as residents of close-in urban neighborhoods, and three times as many of them die in car crashes. Still, millions continue to take flight to the perceived security of suburbia. . . .

The Social Cost of Prosperity

Since 1950, the amount of land in our communities devoted to public uses—parks, civic buildings, schools, churches and so on—decreased by a fifth, while the percentage of income we spend for house mortgages and rental payments increased from a fifth to a full half, according to the American Planning Association. The evidence shows that as we've disinvested in the public areas and "privatized" our lifestyles, we've often left citizenship and care at the front door. So many services are now delivered for a profit by the private sector, we seem to have just gotten out of the habit of taking care of each other.

The 1990s were the most continuously prosperous years in the history of America, as measured in economic terms. Yet Marc Miringoff at Fordham University's Institute for Innovation in Social Policy believes that the trends in his Index of Social Health point to a nation in crisis.

"In 1977," Miringoff says, "social health started its long decline, while the GDP [gross domestic product] continued upward. Since then, the social health index declined forty-five percent while the GDP rose by seventy-nine percent."

When affluenza infects our communities it starts a vicious cycle. We begin to choose things over people, a choice that disconnects us from community life and causes even more consumption, and more disconnection.

Far from being just abstract statistics, the trends he cites are about *real people* in your family and mine, who constitute the social wealth and vigor of our communities. More than three million children are reported abused every year—forty-seven cases for every 1,000 children. Miringoff asks, "What will be the impact on marriage, child rearing, education, and employment from all that abuse?" He also points to youth suicide as an unmistakable indicator of underlying discontent. In 1950, the suicide rate among youth aged fifteen to twenty-four was a relatively low 4.5 per 100,000. By 1970, suicides had almost doubled, and by 1996, the rate was up to twelve. Each suicide resonates far beyond an individual's family, causing serious depression among the victim's friends, schoolmates, and neighbors—not to mention the lost potential of the youth.

When affluenza infects our communities it starts a vicious cycle. We begin to choose things over people, a choice that disconnects us from community life and causes even more consumption, and more disconnection. Health scientists have documented that people in relationships outlive single people, and that people who feel the friendship and support of neighbors need less health care. One study also found that residents of neighborhoods in crisis tend to be clinically "socially" depressed, with lower levels of serotonin—what anti-depressants stimulate—in blood samples.

Have we become a nation too distracted to care? Like the medium-sized fish that ate a small fish, we consume franchise products in the privacy of our homes, then watch helplessly as the big-fish franchise companies bite huge chunks out of our public places, swallowing jobs, traditions, and open space. We assume that someone else is taking care of things—we pay them to take care of things so we can concentrate on working and spending. But to our horror, we discover that many of the service providers, merchandise retailers, and caretakers are not really taking care of us anymore. It might be more appropriate to say they're *consuming* us.

15

Breaking Away from Materialism

Bill Talen

Bill Talen operates the Church of Stop Shopping and has authored What Should I Do If Reverend Billy Is in My Store?

For the average American consumer, resisting making a purchase is an extremely difficult one. Buying fills the void, keeping Americans from thinking about the unknown, the mysteries of life and death. Only by making the brave decision not to buy *can consumers reclaim the "ordinary life," a life open to the mysteries of the unknown. While embracing the unknown may feel strange to the American consumer, it is nonetheless essential to a healthier future.*

In our strange worship at the Church of Stop Shopping we recently took a shiny Sunbeam toaster and put it in the center of the altar.

A young man named Jonah walked up the aisle of the church for his exorcism. As he walked toward the Sunbeam his obvious admiration for it, competing with his faith in the potential of his own buylessness, was very clear. The congregation prayed that he would somehow not grab that sleek chrome bread heater (it resembled a Mercedes coupe and had computerized controls, including a woman's voice that purred "Your toast is done"). I placed my hand on the forehead of this shaking soul as he pleaded with us, "Oh, I don't need your help, I'm just browsing!" How could we possibly blame him for the bald lie? We had positioned the Sunbeam beautifully on a red velvet cloth.

Not-buying is a brave thing to do.

As Jonah reached for the product we prayed hard. The choir hummed and the deacons moved forward to lay hands on the craven consumer as the devil pulled the young man's begging fingers toward the toaster. Jonah was pretty far gone. "Oh . . . toast and butter . . . toast and butter . . . it's more than a smell. . . . Oh, my God! Black currant jam on the butter, oh, oh!" The cry was hideous.

But wait! Jonah's hand hesitated, and then pulling out of that force field, it flew back and wavered there in the air. Jonah stared, in shock, at his released fingers. Then he ran around the church as if proving to a Pentecostal TV audience that now he could walk. Held aloft by the preacher, his hand was shaking with new freedom, unburdened. The Stop Shopping Gospel Choir was swaying with the power of a receiptless God-Goddess that surpasseth all valuation. The object looked cheated, cuck-olded. Finally the Sunbeam deluxe toaster was just . . . junk.

The Temptation to Buy

Not-buying is a brave thing to do. At first it may induce vertigo, identity weirdness, and a desire for an unwanted pregnancy, but most often a new believer will have an abnormal kitsch-acquisition fit. The first response to the break in buying may be a huge sucking sound in your hands—you want to buy something, *anything*. You are headed for a relapse, a spree. My pastoral advice is to steer clear of Ralph Lauren, Kenneth Cole, or any other fashion designer who is trying to anticipate the not-buying revolution by copping a look of weatheredness, offhandedness, or lack of manufacture. Their sales departments think all day about your escape, admiring it and blocking it. They study you via surveillance feeds as they sit in their easy chairs, thoughtfully rubbing their chins.

In the Church of Stop Shopping we believe that buying is not nearly as interesting as not-buying.

When you lift your hand from the product and back away from it, a bright, unclaimed space opens up. Consumers think it is a vacuum. It is really only the *unknown*—full of suppressed ocean life, glitterati from Bosch [manufacturer of home appliances], DNA twists, and childhood quotes that if remembered would burn down the Disney Store. Many Americans consider this withdrawing gesture a dark thing. Officially, it is absurd, an antigesture, like an American who didn't go west, who didn't go into space, who had sex without a car.

The Church of Stop Shopping

In the Church of Stop Shopping we believe that buying is not nearly as interesting as not-buying. When you back away from the purchase, the product may look up at you with wanton eyes, but it will slump quickly back onto the shelf and sit there trying to get a life. The product needs you worse than you need it—remember that.

The bumper sticker says, Birth, Shopping, Death. Well, birth and death are a part of ordinary life.

Now, if you try this—if you lift your hand from the product, pull that hand back into the aisle, back away from the product, and carefully move toward the door—you may feel turbulence deep in your muscles' memory. You may feel the old grab, the lift, the swipe of plastic, and finally the bagging for the road. The ex-consumer can easily lose his or her footing, buffeted by all those ghost gestures.

Like crack cocaine or membership in the National Rifle Association, shopping is an annihilating addiction that must be slowed down to be stopped. Or flooded with new and different light. But people, please—*do something!* Think of something quick. The research phase is over. How many times do we have to hear that seven percent of the world's population is taking a third of the world's resources? How many neighborhoods need to be malled? When will our foreign policy be violent enough to turn our heads? Recently a local Starbucks rang with shouts of "We are from the Church of the Necessary Interruption!" We will try many strategies. Enacting a purchase in a formal church ritual on Sunday or acting out a comic version of being born again might help those parishioners when they are cornered in Temptation Mall. Sweatshops are truly shocking, and I've seen the sheer force of the information stop a shopper. We make dramas, we sing and shout, and we chain ourselves to Mickey Mouse. We are desperate to access the bright and unclaimed space that the corporations must desperately hide.

In another time, long, long ago, maybe you could have gone ahead and had a life without shopping. But now life without shopping is something that takes years of practice, since shopping is so virulent and ubiquitous that mothers are bathing their wombs with the sounds of Mozart so that their fetuses will score higher on their SATs. Now everything from the most intimate disease to daydreaming is a pretext for the avant-fascism of convenience, comfort, and closure.

The Ordinary Life

We might call that unclaimed space "ordinary life." And how do we design that back in? How much of real life hasn't made it into our fully mediated consumption? Can we ever go home again? We have made thousands of purchases—thousands of times the doors have closed behind us as we walked farther into that big, big sale.

The bumper sticker says, Birth, Shopping, Death. Well, birth and death are a part of ordinary life. And ordinary life is itself amazing; the intriguing mystery that precedes birth and follows death does not stop when we are alive. Perhaps the great con began when the churches made us pay for our own arrival and departure. Life itself has as much unknown in it as death; it is just as inexplicable. That's the thrill of the ride. We say, Put the ODD Back in GOD!

We shop because we fear life. We shop because we want to banish from life something we identify with death, the unknown. It waits for us in that bright, unclaimed space. Of course, we are trained to think of what we can't know as a bad thing. Actually, it is the source of the brightness; it is why this space has no owner . . . .

While I'm claiming that the rejection of living-by-products opens up a sensual and peopled life, yet it does have in it an acceptance of the unknown, which is always waiting with the glorious indifference of the fires that float above us in the night sky. Is it a contradiction that accepting this unknown is what makes it possible for us to live together? Well, there is nothing more thoroughly mysterious than love, thank God. Those who organize defenses against the Unknown (such as religious fundamentalists and consumer fundamentalists) foment numbness, hatred, and war. Unfortunately, they have perfected their imitation of ordinary living, and that comes to us as the comforting ghost gesture of shopping.

Ordinary life will feel counterintuitive, to put it mildly. But what will happen to the American consumer when the consuming stops is about as fascinating a question as we can ask.

Organizations to Contact

Adbusters Media Foundation
1234 W. Seventh Ave., Vancouver, BC V6H 1B7
  Canada
(604) 736-9401 • fax: (604) 737-6021
e-mail: info@adbusters.org
Web site: www.adbusters.org

Adbusters is a network of artists, activists, writers, and other people who want to build a new social activist movement. The organization publishes *Adbusters* magazine, which explores the ways that commercialism destroys physical and cultural environments. Spoof ads and information on political action are available on the Web site.

American Enterprise Institute (AEI)
1150 Seventeenth St. NW, Washington, DC 20036
(202) 862-5800 • fax: (202) 862-7177
Web site: www.aei.org

The American Enterprise Institute is a public policy institute that sponsors research and provides commentary on a wide variety of issues, including economics, social welfare, and government tax and regulatory policies. It publishes the bimonthly magazine *American Enterprise* and the *AEI Newsletter*.

Cato Institute
1000 Massachusetts Ave. NW, Washington, DC 20001-5403
(202) 842-0200 • fax: (202) 842-3490
e-mail: cato@cato.org
Web site: www.cato.org

The Cato Institute is a nonpartisan public policy research foundation dedicated to limiting the role of government and protecting individual liberties. It publishes the quarterly magazine *Regulation*, the bimonthly *Cato Policy Report*, and numerous policy papers and articles.

Center for a New American Dream

6930 Carroll Ave., Suite 900, Takoma Park, MD 20912
(301) 891-3683
e-mail: newdream@newdream.org
Web site: www.newdream.org

The Center for a New American Dream is an organization whose goal is to help Americans consume responsibly and thus protect the earth's resources and improve quality of life. Its Kids and Commercialism Campaign provides information on the effects of advertising on children. The center publishes booklets and a quarterly newsletter, *Enough.*

Children's Advertising Review Unit

70 W. Thirty-sixth St., 13th Floor, New York, NY 10018
(866) 334-6272 (ext. 111)
e-mail: caru@caru.bbb.org
Web site: www.caru.org

As the children's branch of the U.S. advertising industry's self-regulation program, the Children's Advertising Review Unit reviews ads aimed at children and promotes responsible children's advertising. It also corrects misleading or inaccurate commercials with the help of advertisers. Commentary and articles are available on the Web site.

Commercial Alert

4110 SE Hawthorne Blvd., #123, Portland, OR 97214
(503) 235-8012 • fax: (503) 235-5073
e-mail: info@commercialalert.org
Web site: www.commercialalert.org

Commercial Alert is a nonprofit organization whose goal is to prevent commercial culture from exploiting children and destroying family and community values. It works toward that goal by conducting campaigns against commercialism in classrooms and marketing to children. News and calls for action against various marketing tactics are posted on the Web site.

Competitive Enterprise Institute (CEI)
1001 Connecticut Ave. NW, Suite 1250, Washington, DC
20036
(202) 331-1010 • fax: (202) 331-0640
e-mail: info@cei.org
Web site: www.cei.org

CEI is a nonprofit public policy organization dedicated to advancing the principles of free enterprise and limited government. It believes that individuals are best helped not by government intervention, but by making their own choices in a free marketplace. CEI's publications include the monthly newsletter *Monthly Planet,* and articles, including "The Winds of Global Change: Which Way Are They Blowing?" and "The Triumph of Democratic Capitalism: The Threat of Global Governance," which are available on its Web site.

Earth Island Institute
300 Broadway, Suite 28, San Francisco, CA 94133
(415) 788-3666 • fax: (415) 788-7324
e-mail: earthisland@earthisland.org
Web site: www.earthisland.org

Earth Island Institute's work addresses environmental issues and their relation to such concerns as human rights and economic development in the third world. The institute's publications include the quarterly *Earth Island Journal.* The articles "Bucking the Corporate Future" and "In Favor of a New Protectionism" are available on its Web site.

Economic Policy Institute (EPI)
1600 L St. NW, Suite 1200, Washington, DC 20036
(202) 775-8810
Web site: www.epinet.org

The Economic Policy Institute conducts research and provides a forum for the exchange of information on economic policy. It promotes educational programs to encourage discussion of economic policy and economic issues, particularly the economics of poverty, unemployment, inflation, American industry, international competitiveness, and problems of economic adjustment as they affect the community and the individual. EPI publishes the *EPI Journal* and the biennial *State of Working America*.

Foundation for Economic Education (FEE)
30 S Broadway, Irvington, NY 10533
(914) 591-7230 • fax: (914) 591-8910
e-mail: freeman@fee.org
Web site: www.fee.org

FEE publishes information and commentary in support of private property, the free market, and limited government. It frequently publishes articles on capitalism and conservatism in its monthly magazine the *Freeman*.

Friends of the Earth
1717 Massachusetts Ave. NW, Suite 600, Washington, DC 20036-2002
(877) 843-8687 • fax: (202) 783-0444
e-mail: foe@foe.org
Web site: www.foe.org

Friends of the Earth is a national advocacy organization dedicated to protecting the planet from environmental degradation; preserving biological, cultural, and ethnic diversity; and empowering citizens to have an influential voice in decisions affecting the quality of their environment. It publishes the quarterly *Friends of the Earth Newsmagazine*, recent and archived issues of which are available on its Web site.

Heritage Foundation
214 Massachusetts Ave. NE, Washington, DC 20002
(202) 546-4400 • fax: (202) 546-0904
e-mail: info@heritage.org
Web site: www.heritage.org

The Heritage Foundation is a conservative think tank that supports the principles of free enterprise and limited government. Its many publications include the quarterly magazine

Policy Review and the occasional paper series *Heritage Talking Points*. On its Web site the foundation includes articles on many issues concerning humanity's future, including globalization

Progressive Policy Institute (PPI)
600 Pennsylvania Ave. SE, Suite 400, Washington, DC 20003
(202) 546-0007 • fax: (202) 544-5014
Web site: www.ppionline.org

PPI is a public policy research organization that strives to develop alternatives to the traditional debate between liberals and conservatives. It advocates economic policies designed to stimulate broad upward mobility and social policies designed to liberate the poor from poverty and dependence. The institute publishes the book *Building the Bridge: 10 Big Ideas to Transform America.*

Reason Foundation
3415 S. Sepulveda Blvd., Suite 400, Los Angeles, CA 90034
(310) 391-2245
Web site: www.reason.org

The foundation works to provide a better understanding of the intellectual basis of a free society and to develop new ideas in public policy making. It researches contemporary social, economic, urban, and political problems. The foundation believes that welfare has become a destructive multigenerational lifestyle that burdens working Americans with higher taxes. It publishes the newsletter *Privatization Watch* monthly and *Reason* magazine eleven times a year.

Worldwatch Institute
1776 Massachusetts Ave. NW, Washington, DC 20036-1904
(202) 452-1999 • fax: (202) 296-7365
e-mail: worldwatch@worldwatch.org
Web site: www.worldwatch.org

Worldwatch is a research organization that analyzes and calls attention to global problems, including environmental concerns such as the loss of cropland, forests, habitat, species, and water supplies. It compiles the annual State of the World anthology and publishes the bimonthly magazine *World Watch* and the World Watch Paper Series, which includes *Home Grown: The Case for Local Food in a Global Market* and *Underfed and Overfed: The Global Epidemic of Malnutrition.*

Bibliography

Books

Tom Bigg, ed.   *Survival for a Small Planet: The Sustainable Development Agenda.* London: Earthscan, 2004.

Lizabeth Cohen   *A Consumers' Republic: The Politics of Mass Consumption in Postwar America.* New York: Knopf, 2003.

Gary Cross   *An All-Consuming Century.* New York: Columbia University Press, 2002.

Pamela Danziger   *Let Them Eat Cake: Marketing Luxury to the Masses—as Well as the Classes.* Chicago: Kaplan, 2005.

John De Graaf, David Wann, and Thomas H. Naylor   *Affluenza: The All-Consuming Epidemic.* San Francisco: Berrett-Koehler, 2002.

Paul Ehrlich and Anne H. Ehrlich   *One with Nineveh: Politics, Consumption, and the Human Future.* Washington, DC: Island Press, 2005.

Robert J. Farrell   *One Nation Under Goods: Malls and the Seduction of American Shopping.* Washington, DC: Smithsonian Books, 2003.

Robert H. Frank   *Luxury Fever: Money and Happiness in an Era of Excess.* Princeton, NJ: Princeton University Press, 2000.

Bruno S. Frey and   *Happiness and Economics: How the Economy and Institutions Affect Human Well-Being.* Princeton, NJ: Princeton University Press, 2001.
Alois Stutzer

Mary Grigsby   *Buying Time and Getting By: The Voluntary Simplicity Movement.* Albany: State University of New York Press, 2004.

Bill Jensen   *Simplicity: The New Competitive Advantage in a World of More, Better, Faster.* New York: Perseus, 2001.

Tim Kasser   *The High Price of Materialism.* Cambridge, MA: MIT Press, 2003.

Robert Lane   *The Loss of Happiness in Market Democracies.* New Haven, CT: Yale University Press, 2001.

Kalle Lasn   *Culture Jam: How to Reverse*
                      America's Suicidal Consumer Binge—
                      and Why We Must. New York:
                      Harper, 2000.

Susan Linn   *Consuming Kids: The Hostile Takeover*
                      of Childhood. New York: New Press,
                      2004.

Bjorn Lomborg   *The Skeptical Environmentalist: Mea-*
                      suring the Real State of the World.
                      London: Cambridge University Press,
                      2001.

Vincent J. Miller   *Consuming Religion: Christian Faith*
                      and Practice in a Consumer Culture.
                      London: Continuum International,
                      2003.

Murray Milner   *Freaks, Geeks, and Cool Kids: Ameri-*
                      can Teenagers, Schools, and the Cul-
                      ture of Consumption. New York: Rou-
                      tledge, 2004.

Jon Pahl   *Shopping Malls and Other Sacred*
                      Spaces: Putting God in Place. Grand
                      Rapids, MI: Brazos Press, 2003.

Thomas Princen, Michael F. Maniates, and Ken Conca, eds. — *Confronting Consumption.* Cambridge, MA: MIT Press, 2003.

George Ritzer — *The McDonaldization of Society.* London: Pine Forge Press, 2004.

Juliet B. Schor — *Born to Buy: The Commercialized Child and the New Consumer Culture.* New York: Scribner, 2004.

Barry Schwartz — *The Paradox of Choice: Why Less Is More.* New York: HarperPerennial, 2005.

James B. Twitchell — *Lead Us into Temptation: The Triumph of American Materialism.* New York: Columbia University Press, 2000.

James B. Twitchell — *Living It Up: America's Love Affair with Luxury.* New York: Simon & Schuster, 2003.

Paco Underhill — *Call of the Mall: The Geography of Shopping.* New York: Simon & Schuster, 2004.

Paco Underhill   *Why We Buy: The Science of Shopping*. New York: Simon & Schuster, 2000.

Peter C. Whybrow *American Mania: When More Is Not Enough*. New York: W.W. Norton, 2005.

Sharon Zukin   *Point of Purchase: How Shopping Changed American Culture*. New York: Routledge, 2003.

Periodicals

David Landis Barnhill "Good Work: An Engaged Buddhist Response to the Dilemmas of Consumerism," *Buddhist-Christian Studies*, 2004.

Daniel Benjamin "The Eight Myths of Recycling," *American Enterprise*, January/February 2004.

Hana Boivie "Buy Nothing: Improve Everything," *Humanist*, November/December 2003.

Bruce Bower "Buyer Beware," *Science News*, September 1, 2003.

Philip Camill — "Watch Your Step: The Impacts of Personal Consumption on the Environment," *Journal of College Science Teaching*, September 2002.

William T. Cavanaugh — "When Enough Is Enough: Why God's Abundant Life Won't Fit in a Shopping Cart, and Other Mysteries of Consumerism," *Sojourners*, May 2005.

Lisabeth Cohen — "The Politics of Mass Consumption in America," *Chronicle of Higher Education*, January 3, 2003.

Geoffrey Colvin — "Admit It: You, Too, Are Paris Hilton," *Fortune*, December 22, 2003.

Dinesh D'Souza — "What's So Great About America?" *American Enterprise*, April/May 2002.

Gregg Easterbrook — "The Real Truth About Money: Why We Remain Keen for Green Even Though It Often Gives Us More Social Anxiety than Satisfaction," *Time*, January 17, 2005.

Brian Fuller — "Consumer as King: A Benign Tyrant?" *Electronic Engineering Times*, November 1, 2004.

Gary Gardner   "Hungry for More: Re-Engaging Religious Teachings on Consumption," *World Watch*, September/October 2005.

Lawrence B. Glickman   "The 'Ism' That Won the Century," *Nation*, December 4, 2000.

Gloria Gonzalez   "Consumerism Brings Savings, Member Satisfaction," *Business Insurance*, June 28, 2004.

Dana Hudepohl   "Living Below Your Means," *Organic Style*, September 2004.

Katharine Isbell   "Ethical Consumerism," *Green Teacher*, Summer 2003.

Victoria James   "Rubbish," *Geographical*, September 2005.

John F. Kavanaugh   "Consuming Christmas," *America*, December 19, 2005.

Katy Kelly and Linda Kulman   "Kid Power," *U.S. News & World Report*, September 13, 2004.

Paul Kingsnorth   "The Gospel According to Billy (Reverend Billy)," *Ecologist*, October 2003.

Michael
McCarthy

"Shopping 'Til We Drop: Can Psychology Save Us from Our Lust for Possessions?" *Lancet*, January 24, 2004.

Deirdre N.
McCloskey

"Capital Gains: How Economic Growth Benefits the World," *Christian Century*, May 4, 2004.

Patrick
McCormick

"Dying of Consumption: Four New Books Examine the Dangers of Consumerism and Show How Americans Are Getting Less from Our 'Buy More' Culture," *U.S. Catholic*, April 2004.

Leah McLaren

"Shopping Is Not Just for Christmas," *Spectator*, December 14, 2002.

Sharda Prashad

"Flaunting It: It's Not Just About Owning the Rolex, Lamborghini or Vuitton. It's About Others Noticing," *Toronto Star*, May 15, 2005.

Matthew Price

"Weary of the Leisure Class; What Would Thorstein Veblen, Who Took No Prisoners in His 'Theory of the Leisure Class,' Make of Today's Consumer Culture?" *Boston Globe*, December 12, 2004.

Gary Ruskin   "The Fast Food Trap: How Commer-
                       cialism Creates Overweight Chil-
                       dren," *Mothering*, November/
                       December 2003.

Robert J.   "Shop 'Til We Drop?" *Wilson Quar-
Samuelson   terly*, Winter 2004.

Miranda Sawyer   "Consuming Passions," *New States-
                       man*, January 20, 2003.

Jennifer   "The Changing Badges of Status with
Steinhauer   Expensive Services, Consumption Is
                       Less Conspicuous Class in America,"
                       International Herald Tribune, May 30,
                       2005.

Jennifer   "When the Joneses Wear Jeans," *New
Steinhauer   York Times*, May 29, 2005.

David Wann   "Does Our Disposable Consumer
                       Culture Consume So Much of Our
                       Time That We Have Precious Little
                       Left for What's Really Important in
                       Life?" *Denver Post*, August 3, 2003.

Michael Warren   "Spirituality and Wealth: The Bur-
                       dens of Silence," *Catholic New Times*,
                       June 20, 2004.

Emil A. Wcela   "A Dangerous Common Enemy Fighting the Great God Stuff," *America*, February 21, 2005.

Alan Wolfe   "America Consumed by Consumption," *New Republic*, October 23, 2000.

Index